Contents

Executive Summary

WMEB Consultants, in partnership with Karen Ross of the University of Birmingham's School of Continuing Studies, were commissioned by ALBSU (The Adult Literacy and Basic Skills Unit) in November 1993 to undertake a study to examine the effectiveness of basic skills training in the workplace.

The research set out specifically to examine:

i) *The contribution which workplace training can make to improving the basic skills of an individual or group of individuals.*

ii) *The impact that this has on their performance at work and, in turn, upon the performance of the company or employer.*

iii) *Any indirect benefits of the programme – for example in enhancing levels of self confidence – and the impact of these on the individual's quality of life, both within and outside the workplace.*

Our research methodology is described in detail in section 3 of this report. In summary it was based upon a detailed assessment of 17 individual employer based case study examples.

From these assessments it became clear that the impact of basic skills training and support was closely related to the context within which the potential benefits of the training programme were perceived by the company. Issues of company awareness and commitment were therefore critical factors contributing to the relative effectiveness of the programme.

This led us to develop a broad typology of company involvement in the provision of basic skills support to their employees which is set out in section 4. The range of experiences across the 17 individual case studies is highly disparate. We have therefore set our analysis of case study findings within the framework of this typology as we believe it provides the most rational context for considering their implications.

The typology is based upon three models of company involvement:

- **the employee centred model** – where the company believes that all employees should be accorded opportunities for individual advancement per se, rather than as a means of achieving specific work based objectives

- **the company strategy model** – where basic skills training and support has been identified as a critical component in the achievement of corporate goals, often within the context of a wider business plan for upskilling the workforce and increasing production efficiency

- **the problem centred model** – where the need for basic skills training support has been identified as a result of a specific issue or difficulty facing the company.

We highlight the relationship of the company strategy model to initiatives such as Investors in People and Total Quality Management, and argue that it is within the context of this model that all round effectiveness in terms of the benefits to employee and company can be maximised.

Drawing together some of the operational issues arising from the case studies, we highlight in section 5 a series of practical points concerning the delivery of basic skills training. In doing so we highlight some ways in which apparent constraints may be overcome in order to maximise effectiveness.

Our conclusions are in three parts. Firstly we emphasise that virtually all the case studies examined demonstrated a high degree of effectiveness within the (sometimes limited) objectives set. Secondly we highlight the particular benefits of the company strategy model. In the third part of our conclusions we consider effectiveness in the context of national policy objectives, specifically the achievement of the National Targets for Education and Training, and the drive towards improving industrial competitiveness. We stress the important contribution which the employee centred model can play in the achievement of National Targets. This means large companies can provide important opportunities for substantial sections of the adult population to access essential foundation skills.

In relation to Department of Trade and Industry led initiatives based upon improving competitiveness, we refer to the acknowledged importance of upskilling the workforce, and the Total Quality Management approach. These require the involvement of the whole workforce as part of a holistic approach to the development of human resources within a well defined corporate strategy. We stress the critical nature of basic skills support in this process, particularly communication skills. We highlight the fact that new structures such as Quality Circles will not function effectively unless individuals are equipped with the requisite inter-personal and communication skills to enable them to make a full contribution.

Finally we consider how the positive benefits of basic skills training in the workplace might be extended. The major issue that we highlight is one of management awareness and perceptions. This problem is highly pervasive. It includes a lack of knowledge (i) about the extent of basic skills within their own workforce; (ii) about the effect which this has on company performance and the achievement of corporate goals; (iii) about the sources of help in this area, and of the methods of flexibly delivering such training and minimising disruption to production; and finally (iv) about the potential benefits which can accrue. The need to increase the overall level of awareness of companies forms a major theme in our recommendations.

Part 1

Conducts and Analysis of the Research

1 Introduction

It is widely recognised that the lack of an adequately trained workforce is a major factor inhibiting the competitiveness of British industry. A basic level of competence in written, number, communication and language skills is an essential foundation for more advanced training. Despite this, few companies perceive the relevance of basic skills training or have an awareness of the needs of their workforce in this area. The provision of basic skills training in the workplace is therefore still a relatively rare occurrence.

The Pilot Projects funded under the Basic Skills at Work Programme, which was managed by ALBSU (The Adult Literacy and Basic Skills Unit) and commenced in 1991, provided the opportunity to undertake a detailed examination of a series of case studies based upon specific training programmes within individual companies. These case studies gave an opportunity to assess the impact of this training upon the performance of the individual trainee and of the company.

This report sets out the findings of this research. In view of the fact that some company case studies contain sensitive information, the names of the companies concerned have been anonymised with the use of letter references in this version for publication.

We consider the outcomes of this research to be highly relevant to all those involved in promoting company involvement in education and training, and in seeking to improve the competitiveness of the UK's industrial base.

During the course of this study we have received an extremely high level of co-operation from managers, supervisors, employees, and training providers, and representatives of sponsoring TECs. We would like to thank everybody who participated for the many hours of their valuable time which they contributed so willingly to this project.

2 Basic Skills at Work Programme – Background

2.1 Low Levels of Investment in Training

The costs to industry of not training employees have been widely acknowledged for more than a decade. A number of authoritative studies carried out in the 1980s demonstrated that when compared to her immediate competitors, Britain consistently performed less well on a number of indices including extent of training (see, for example, *Coopers & Lybrand, 1985; Constable and McCormick, 1987; Handy, 1987*). All these studies came to the same gloomy conclusion; British industry either improved its record on training or else risked losing precious market share.

Within manufacturing industries, the demise of the Engineering Industry Training Board meant that there was no longer a penalty on companies if they failed to implement training programmes. Recent studies (for example, *Ross, 1992*) have found that for small and medium sized enterprises (SMEs) in particular, the removal of sanctions has contributed to a reduction in training provision, with companies reporting that they are too busy getting the product through the door to bother about training.

2.2 The Lack of Basic Skills within the Workforce

ALBSU define basic skills as

"the ability to read, write and speak in English and use mathematics at a level necessary to function and progress at work and in society in general".

In Britain, in 1993, ALBSU estimated that about 16 per cent of the adult population had reading or writing difficulties and more than half of these adults were either in work or looking for work. Any improvement in the overall competence of the UK workforce must pay attention to employees' basic skills. Without them, individuals cannot progress satisfactorily at work, often do not benefit from retraining and if they become unemployed, find it difficult to get back into the workforce (ALBSU, 1993a). Once considered primarily an educational issue, lack of proficiency in literacy and numeracy has now become a crucial concern for business.

Changes in the nature of jobs and the composition of the work force have begun to highlight the need for workplace literacy programmes and have encouraged companies to reassess what skills they require from their workforce. Despite current high levels of unemployment, skill shortages are still apparent in many areas and appear likely to grow as the economy expands post recession. In an environment of continuing skills shortages, companies are increasingly having to look to their existing workforce to provide the skills they need and are highlighting skills deficits amongst their staff.

In areas where skill shortages are currently less apparent, and the growth of structural unemployment has led to intense competition for jobs, there is evidence of a tightening of recruitment criteria by companies in an attempt to "sieve out" applicants without basic skills. During the course of our research we identified examples of quite onerous tests required of applicants for fairly low level jobs in terms of verbal reasoning and numberwork.

2.3 The Impact of Technological and Organisational Change

New competitive conditions in the global marketplace are placing new and different demands on workers at all levels within companies. The introduction of new technology, quality related systems such as statistical process control, and organisational restructuring with a greater emphasis on teamworking, all require much higher levels of technical, conceptual and communication skills. These skills are required not just at managerial and technical levels, but are seen as being of increasing relevance to supervisors and operatives (see for example Berry 1991 – "Managing the Total Quality Transformation")

The recent DTI White Paper on "Competitiveness – Helping Business to Win" places significant emphasis on the need to upskill the workforce as part of a drive to achieve "world class standards". The related series of publications – "Managing in the '90s", highlights the relevance of the work of the so-called `Quality Gurus' – Deming, Juran, Taguchi, Ishikawa and others – to the achievement of these standards. Following the methods adopted by the Japanese, most Total Quality Management Programmes extensively employ teamwork to provide improved planning analysis and problem solving, communication, motivation and collective responsibility.

These approaches demand a radical culture change amongst many traditional companies. Elements of this change involve the breaking down of traditional vertical and horizontal barriers which exist within organisations, a move away from a culture of conflict and blame apportionment to one of constructive critical appraisal of issues, and planned prevention rather than detection and correction of faults. Critical in this process is the education, training and empowerment of shopfloor personnel in order to enable them to realise their potential contribution to improving quality and productive efficiency. Supervisory and operative personnel in particular have often previously had few resources invested in their training, and may frequently lack the basic skills necessary to cope with new organisational structures and responsibilities.

2.4 Basic Skill Needs

What, then, are the factors which come into play when considering basic skills training in the workplace? Evaluative research undertaken in Canada (National Literacy Secretariat, 1992) has clear relevance to Britain's education and training environment and findings from this work suggests the following:

- employee training is an important part of business competitiveness but, in a world of tight resources, there is little evidence of organisations' commitment to basic skills development

- organisations which have high quality management systems appear to respond very positively when problems with basic skills deficiencies in the workplace are identified

- changes in technology and operating methods place new demands on the skills of employees, sometimes leading to the development of remedial programmes

- in a unionised environment, employee training is not a problem because it is recognised that there are benefits to everyone

- organisations which are restructuring (downsizing) may see the extent of basic skills problems increase as younger, better educated/skilled and more expensive workers are made redundant and the proportion of skilled to unskilled jobs increases

- rapidly growing organisations can ensure that they do not experience basic skills problems by implementing more rigorous recruitment and selection processes.

Although there are a number of different definitions of workplace (il)literacy, it is clear from those studies which have looked at basic skills needs, that the context and focus of training programmes is important. The kinds of skills needed in the workplace include basic literacy and numeracy but oral communication is also increasingly important in the workplace environment. A useful model which describes the way in which the basic building blocks of literacy and numeracy are an essential foundation to subsequent learning is provided by Carnevae, Gainer and Meltzer (1989):

1. learning to learn

2. reading, writing and computation

3. oral communication and listening

4. creative thinking and problem solving

5. personal management (self-esteem, goal setting, motivation, personal/career development)

6. group effectiveness (interpersonal skills, negotiation, teamwork)

7. organisational effectiveness and leadership.

Whilst some of the more complex skills defined above may exceed a traditional definition of basic skills, the point to make is that all skills require a good basic foundation. Some commentators argue that for skills training at work to be effective, it must be taught in a workplace context, since programmes which offer basic skills training prior to and/or separately from any relevant vocational training schemes have often produced poor results (Sticht, 1989).

However, this is by no means an accepted orthodoxy and it might be that the vocational orientation of training programmes, or relevance to particular working environments, might be of greater importance. Although research on the relationship between job performance and basic skills has produced varied results, there is some agreement that it is more important for workers to be able to apply basic skills in a job performance context than to demonstrate abilities through formal testing procedures (Thiel, 1985).

The functional context of basic skills training is therefore crucial to effective learning, as is understanding the needs of different groups of learners. Several levels of basic skills deficits can be identified (Mikulecky, 1989): firstly, extremely low level ability individuals who need longterm and intensive adult literacy support; a second group are workers whose limited ability in maths, reading, writing, computer literacy or study skills hinders their ability to take advantage of available education and training opportunities; third are workers who need job-related support to enable them to execute particular tasks, gain promotion and/or avoid making dangerous or costly mistakes. Short term basic skills training is often aimed at the accomplishment of specific tasks for particular goals, such as reading charts, improving report writing skills or understanding the principles of statistical process control.

Those organisations which have implemented programmes of basic skills training have been able to identify positive outcomes from programme participation. A large scale study of SMEs in America, for example, found that in those companies where basic skills training had been provided, workplace education programmes provided a simple and economical solution to the problem of training workers with low basic skills (Chisman, 1992). Another study the following year indicated the existence of a specific connection between basic skills training and improvements in productivity, citing one company which reported a 95 per cent reduction in costs resulting from worker mistakes and a doubling of productivity since the company adopted an aggressive education and training programme (BCEL, 1993). Basic skills training which includes elements of English for Speakers of Other Languages (ESOL) have also achieved significant results, and work by Hemphill suggests that such programmes produce a number of outcomes: learners perceive substantial gains in language and literacy proficiency and some gains in productivity; companies perceive the same gains and also identify a link between the two (Hemphill, 1992).

In an effort to establish levels of basic skills difficulties in the workplace (as perceived by companies) and to quantify and describe the costs to companies of such deficits, ALBSU also commissioned Gallup to conduct a survey of UK based companies (ALBSU, 1993b). Overall, most companies in the study did not perceive that basic skills problems among staff have an effect on their organisation, possibly because they believe that their own employees are sufficiently skilled for the jobs they are expected to do.

Of those companies which did recognise adverse effects, 4 per cent mentioned errors, mistakes, and/or competence in job restricted; 3 per cent reported a lack of efficiency and/or professionalism; and 3 per cent mentioned timewasting and/or not being able to get on with the job. When firms were prompted, however, a quarter agreed that basic skills problems amongst staff had resulted in their recruiting from outside their organisation rather than promote internally and a similar proportion agreed that poor basic skills restricted worker flexibility. In terms of hard cash, Gallup estimate that the cost of basic skills deficits to UK industry is more than £4.8 billion each year and on average, poor basic skills cost about £165,000 in poor quality control, lost orders and additional supervisory time to every company which employs more than 50 people.

The importance of workplace literacy has been underscored by an undeniable (albeit sometimes hard to determine) link between basic skills and productivity. Daily reading is now a requirement of almost every job and increasing numbers of jobs demand high levels of education. In 1991, as part of the Basic Skills at Work Programme, ALBSU commissioned the Institute of Manpower Studies to conduct a survey to establish the standard of basic skills (reading, writing, oral communication and numeracy) required of employees in a range of jobs (Atkinson & Spilsbury, 1993). Key findings from this study included the importance of having a firm basic skills foundation on which to build more technical and sophisticated competencies.

The research suggested that the range of jobs open to jobseekers with poor basic skills is very small and shrinking. At the same time, the emphasis placed on good basic skills as a pre-requisite for career development and promotion at work means that they will remain at a premium for people in work as well as jobseekers. What has become clear through numerous research studies is that what might have been an acceptable level of basic skills in the past is no longer good enough for today's businesses. The nature of work has changed and the basic skills of the workforce must change too as companies see higher standards as a crucial key to competitive success. An increasing emphasis on good reading and writing skills is matched by desired improvements in oral communication and associated skills such as teamworking, all of which are regarded as necessary skills for a flexible workforce.

The Basic Skills at Work Programme commenced in April 1991. The programme was managed by ALBSU and funded by the Employment Department, the Department for Education and the Welsh Office. The aims of the Programme were to:

- **encourage partnerships between Training and Enterprise Councils (TECs) and local education and training providers concerning basic skills training.**

- **provide an opportunity to add value to the existing contributions of TECs and education and training providers in this area.**

- **develop new approaches to basic skills training for unemployed adults and employees unable to make progress at work because of difficulties with basic skills.**

The Basic Skills at Work Programme had the following elements: local surveys of the basic skills required by companies commissioned through IMS (see above); surveys of existing vocationally related basic skills provision and pilot projects intended to explore new methods of providing basic skills for both unemployed adults and those in work.

As we go on to describe in the following section, this research is intended to extend current knowledge concerning the effectiveness of programmes of work based basic skills support, based upon a series of case study examples.

3 The Research Methods Used

3.1 Case Studies and their Selection

It was agreed at the outset that our research should be based upon an empirical assessment of the outcomes of a series of case studies of work based training. For practical convenience these case studies were drawn from the range of company-based training programmes funded by ALBSU under the Basic Skills at Work Pilot Programme.

The numbers of individual companies covered by projects funded under the Pilot Programme varied greatly – from single large companies to ten or more small/medium companies.

In selecting which companies to visit our objective was to obtain a reasonably varied sample, thus ensuring that we were able to draw upon contrasting circumstances and approaches in our analysis.

Some of the key criteria used in sample selection were as follows:

Company Type

- public/private sector
- service/manufacturing industry
- small/medium/large in terms of number of employees

Type of Training

- ESOL
- communication skills
- linked to vocational provision or not
- formally accredited or not.

Location of Training

Start Date/Length of Training

All of the above information, where obtainable, was plotted on a matrix from which we selected our sample for detailed assessment. Some revision to this sample was necessary as our work proceeded – due to the departure of key personnel within companies or training providers, or due to practical problems in obtaining information.

The sample was never intended to be representative of the body of companies/employees with basic skills training needs. It is not relevant to talk of 'representative' company samples given the context within which basic skills training has developed.

It is clear that the Pilot Projects themselves did not cover a representative cross section of companies. Under the terms of the programme local TECs/LEAs were asked to identify companies fairly quickly, therefore companies included have tended to be those with whom there was already a close relationship and/or those who had a clear and identified need in the area.

We are confident, however, that our final sample of 17 company based training programmes provides a sufficient variety of approaches to basic skills training, and includes a sufficiently varied mix of companies, to enable meaningful comparisons to be made.

There are of course limits to the degree that observations from a relatively small sample can be inferred as being representative of the wider base of companies. In setting out our conclusions we have borne this very much in mind. We have however been able to supplement this with our own extensive knowledge of training requirements across employer sectors, together with background material supplied by ALBSU, and copies of local evaluations of Pilot Projects which we have not had the opportunity to visit.

3.2 The Characteristics of the Chosen Sample

As intended, the sample chosen provided a varied cross section of companies and approaches. Companies ranged in size from 9000 employees to 4 employees. Numbers of employees involved ranged from 1 to 300 and training hours per individual from 5 to 50. A range of industrial sectors were deliberately targeted, although the Pilot Projects themselves were skewed towards manufacturing rather than service sector companies.

Three service sector employees were included in the sample: a company administering cleaning contracts, a Nursing Home, and a Health Authority. Manufacturing companies varied greatly in terms of size and product area: the latter included chemicals, pallet repair and manufacture, electronic equipment, rubber components for cars, multi-terrain vehicle assembly, and diving equipment.

Roughly 80% of the sample provided formal accreditation through units of Wordpower or Numberpower, the City & Guilds awards in Communication Skills and Numeracy, for some or all participants. It is difficult to generalise about course content as all courses attempted to respond to individual employee needs. However in general terms, five examples were primarily orientated towards literacy skills, three emphasised literacy and communication skills, six literacy and numeracy skills, two focused upon oral communication skills. In three examples a significant component involved addressing the particular needs of ethnic minority workers arising as a result of language difficulties.

Two of the programmes were delivered away from the workplace, and one partly on and partly off site. The more substantive off site programme was delivered a short bus ride from the factory and employees were bussed in for the training as a group after clocking in.

3.3 Assessing Effectiveness in the Context of Individual Case Studies

A carefully structured and uniform approach to the evaluation of the impact of each training programme was developed, based upon a standard interview pro-forma used in all case study interviews. The approach adopted is one developed by WMEB Consultants based upon the Treasury model ("Policy Evaluation for Managers" – HM Treasury) and used successfully elsewhere on behalf of the Employment Department and numerous Training and Enterprise Councils.

Wherever possible, interviews were held with the following individuals:

i)   **a sample of employees**

ii)   **supervisors or line managers**

iii)   **senior managers**

iv)   **training providers.**

Interviews with training providers provided a background or context within which the assessments took place.

Where available, information was gathered from each of the three groups under the following heads:

1. **Initial Objectives/Expectations about training outputs and outcomes** – as far as companies were concerned this involved an evaluation of the factors which motivated the company to participate in the programme and how they expected to benefit corporately. Employees were asked what they had hoped to gain as individuals from the training.

2. **'Baseline' information on the capabilities of employees before undertaking the training** – where written assessments of individuals had been undertaken prior to the training these were referred to.

3. **Immediate outputs and ultimate outcomes** – this included: impact on the skills of the individual employee in terms of his/her immediate work tasks, impact upon wider workplace skills – team working, motivation, participation, impact on wider life skills, impact upon work performance – in terms of the employees individually and collectively, aggregate impact on company performance.

3.4 The Quality and Interpretation of Data

Assessments of the effectiveness of any activities are always much more difficult where there is a dearth of quantitative data. The fact that our evaluation was post-hoc meant that we did not have the opportunity to become involved in setting up quantitative indicators at the outset of the programmes. Thus, aside from the standard administrative and financial management information required by ALBSU to ensure accountability, we have been largely reliant upon the subjective impressions of those involved in order to assess effectiveness. Only two companies contacted considered themselves in a position to make some crude estimate of the impact of the training on turnover. The failure of companies to systematically evaluate the costs and benefits of training programmes is symptomatic of a wider lack of awareness of training needs and potential benefits.

Despite the limited amount of quantitative information we have no doubt that where we have identified benefits these were real and accurate. The scale of these benefits, and their impact on the bottom line efficiency of employing enterprises has unavoidably been based on a synthesis of individual perceptions rather than on directly measurable indicators. Such indicators are in any case fraught with difficulties of interpretation – particularly the problem of attribution in circumstances where multiple training programmes are underway simultaneously, and where companies are in the midst of organisational changes or changes in production systems.

We were aware that many of our respondents, as recipients of external assistance, or as participants or `torchbearers' for the programme may have felt it necessary to put a positive gloss on outcomes. We attempted to overcome this potential problem in two ways – firstly by stressing at the outset that we wanted an `honest' response, and secondly, wherever possible, by seeking corroboration from a relatively disinterested party. In manufacturing concerns the latter was often a production manager, an individual who typically had potentially much to lose as a result of any disruptive effect of the training, yet was also able to comment objectively on its benefits to the company.

3.5 Supplementary Information

As we have indicated, information from the 17 case study companies was supplemented with a range of background information and survey reports supplied by ALBSU, and a number of in-depth evaluations of local projects carried out independently by local TECs and training providers. All of this material has been analysed to produce the conclusions and recommendations contained in this report.

Figure 1: Summary Analysis of Case Study Data and Outcomes

Notes

1. Trainees on the programme assessed
2. Principal areas covered:
   WP – Wordpower
   NP – Numberpower
   C – Communication skills
   ESOL – English for speakers of other languages
3. O.L. – Open learning
4. Degree of achievement based on interviews:
   H – High
   M – Medium
   L – Low
5. Value placed on benefits of programme:
   H – High
   M – Medium
   L – Low

Company	Total No. of employees on Site	No. of Trainees (note 1)	Curriculum (note 2)	Company Based./Indiv. Centred	Voluntary/Compulsory Attendance	No. Hours/Trainee (note 3)	Formally Accredited? YES/NO	On site or Off site training	Ability to perform current task	Ability to cope with new tasks	Increase in confidence	Improved team working	Communication with Snr. Mgt.	Life skills improved	Career enhanced/redundancy avoided	Increased Productivity	Quality improved	Ideas/Suggestions	Team working	Statutory/customer requirements met	Foundation for Further Training	Training/Personnel Manager	Line Manager(s)	Senior Management
A	1100	11	WP C	C	C	37	ON	Y	H	H	H	H	H	M	M	M	H	M	M	M	H	H	H	H
B	1000	300	WP NP	C	V	VARIED	ON	Y	H	H	H	H	M	M	L	H	H	M	M	M	M	H	H	H
C	745	10	WP	C/I	V	VARIED	ON	Y	M	M	H	M	L	H	L	M	M	H	M	L	M	H	M	L
D	9000	30	W/N	I	V	VARIED	ON	Y	M	M	H	M	L	H	L	M	M	H	M	L	M	H	M	L
E	55	12	ESOL	C	C	5	ON	N	L	L	M	L	L	H	H	L	M	H	L	H	H	M	M	M
F	370	8	C	C	C	16	ON	N	H	H	M	M	H	H	L	M	M	M	H	M	H	H	H	H
G	70	12	WP C	C/I	C	5	OFF	Y	M	M	M	M	H	H	L	H	M	M	H	H	H	H	H	H
H	2010	150	WP C	C/I	V	VARIED	ON/OFF	Y	M	M	M	M	M	H	H	L	L	M	L	L	M	H	H	H
I	3200	29	WP	C	V	15	ON	Y	H	H	H	L	M	H	M	M	H	M	H	L	M	H	H	H
J	400	25	WP	C/I	V	12	ON	Y	M	N/A	M	L	L	H	L	L	M	M	M	L	M	H	M	N/A
K	320	1	WP NP	I	V	12	ON	Y	H	M	H	L	M	H	M	M	M	M	L	L	M	H	M	N/A
L	4	1	WP	I	V	O.L.	OFF	N	M	M	M	M	H	H	H	M	M	M	H	H	H	N/A	H	N/A
M	22	2	WP	C/I	V	15	ON	Y	H	M	H	M	M	M/H	H	M	M	M	M	L	M	N/A	H	H
N	82	28	WP NP	C/I	V	O.L.	OFF	Y	M	M	H	L	L	H	M	M	M	M	M	L	H	N/A	N/A	N/A
O	6000	299	WP NP/C	C/I	V	VARIED	ON	Y	M	L	H	M	M	M	L	L	M	H	M	H	M	H	H	H
P	500	70	WP NP	C	V	50	ON	Y	M	M	H	M	M	M	H	L	L	H	M	L	M	H	H	N/A
Q	260	17	C	C	V	36	ON	Y	L	L	M	L	L	M	L	L	L	H	L	L	M	M	N/A	H

4 The Background to Basic Skills at Work

4.1 The Case Study Outcomes

Figure 1 summarises in tabular form some of the key characteristics of the sample of case studies together with key outcomes. Outcomes are summarised in very broad terms in Figure 1 – H, M and L standing for the level of impact (High/Medium/Low) which the training was assessed to have achieved in the relevant area, based upon the interview responses.

As is reflected in the descriptions of individual projects attached as Appendix 1, all of the projects were considered to have been effective in terms of the objectives set for them at the outset. These perceptions were common to both employees and intermediate layers of management, although in a small number of cases there was concern that the achievements were not fully appreciated by senior management.

The varying levels of impact reflected in Figure 1 therefore arise as a result of the fact that the targeted objectives of the different projects varied considerably. Some projects for example, were designed to overcome a very specific and immediate problem, whereas others were of a more fundamental and wide ranging nature.

A notable feature of virtually all case study examples was the enthusiasm demonstrated by the employees. The fact that companies had seen fit to provide training for lower graded staff was often of itself a strong motivator. It was clear that at the outset many employees were intimidated by the prospect of training and of 'making a fool of themselves' infront of a wider group. In all cases however, as the training progressed, the practical realisation that they were able to cope with the tasks provided a very considerable and permanent boost to self-confidence. In view of the fact that they contain certain sensitive information, the case studies have been rendered anonymous by describing individual companies merely as 'Company A' or 'Company G', both in the subsequent discussion, and in the case studies in Part Two of this report.

4.2 Overview – The Development of a Typology

Having considered the question of impact and effectiveness on an individual project basis, it is important to try to identify common factors which contribute to wider effectiveness.

Effectiveness can be defined as:

❝The extent to which the objectives of a policy are achieved without reference to cost. The most effective policy being one which achieves all its objectives.❞

Policy Evaluation: A Guide for Managers – HM Treasury

Objectives can be "strategic" i.e. concerned with significantly improving the overall performance of the company/agency, and/or individuals; or "operational" i.e. concerned with resolving an immediate problem or issue.

In most of the case studies we examined, objectives were not explicitly documented at the outset and had to be teased out during the course of our discussions. Additionally, in the case of a number of the more successful projects it was clear that the training had contributed to the achievement of additional objectives not envisaged as being relevant at the outset – enhanced team working and increased employee motivation, for example.

Within our case studies the range of objectives set by companies for basic skills training programmes varied considerably. In some cases the primary (strategic) objective was the self-advancement of the employee or improving the competitiveness of the company. In other cases (operational) objectives were focused upon resolving a specific difficulty or complying with an externally imposed standard. Whereas most of the examples we investigated could demonstrate a large measure of effectiveness on their own terms (ie in relation to the achievement of the – sometimes fairly narrow – range of objectives set by the companies), a more limited number of projects were able to demonstrate the achievement of a range of wider objectives.

It is clearly important to try to assess the distinguishing features of those projects which had been most effective in successfully achieving a range of high level objectives. However, an initial cursory examination of the results of our case study assessments and other material indicated a wide diversity in forms of delivery, costs and effectiveness, reflecting the diversity of our sample, with little apparent correlation between the factors contributing to effectiveness. However, when we came to analyse our results in more detail it became clear that, in most cases the organisation, delivery, impact and effectiveness of the programmes were highly reflective of the initial motivating factor behind employer involvement. This is perhaps unsurprising, as all of the programmes examined had been developed in response to the often partial employer perceptions of company or workforce needs, rather than any comprehensive training needs assessment.

Arising from this, by drawing upon the case studies we were able to develop a broad typology of company involvement in basic skills training provision (see Figure 2 overleaf). By locating our case studies within this framework (see Figure 3) we have been able to provide a structured analysis of how they have developed as well as how effective they have been in

Figure 2: Typology of Company Involvement in Basic Skills Training

Model	Reason for Involvement	Focus of Training	Voluntary/ Compulsory	Course Content	Impact on Company Performance	Outcomes	Examples
Employee Centred	General desire to 'uplift' workforce and promote an education/training culture	Personal development	Entirely voluntary	Broad-individual centred	Beneficial but limited	Trainees benefit as individuals, company benefit less tangible	Company C Company D
Company Strategy	Training viewed as a specific and integral part of corporate planning	Maximisation of individual contribution to corporate goals through increased responsibility	By agreement but pressure to attend	Company and individual centred	Very significant	Trainees benefit as individuals and company benefits as a result of increased performance and team working	Company F Company G
Problem Centred	Specific difficulty or issue impacting upon company performance identified as being due to lack of basic skills	Enabling individuals to perform assigned tasks more efficiently	Compulsory	Company centred	Limited	Problem solved, but individual potential not fully realised	Company E Company I

meeting firstly, the objectives established by the individuals and companies at the outset of the programme, and secondly, a series of other desirable objectives which may not have been apparent at the outset.

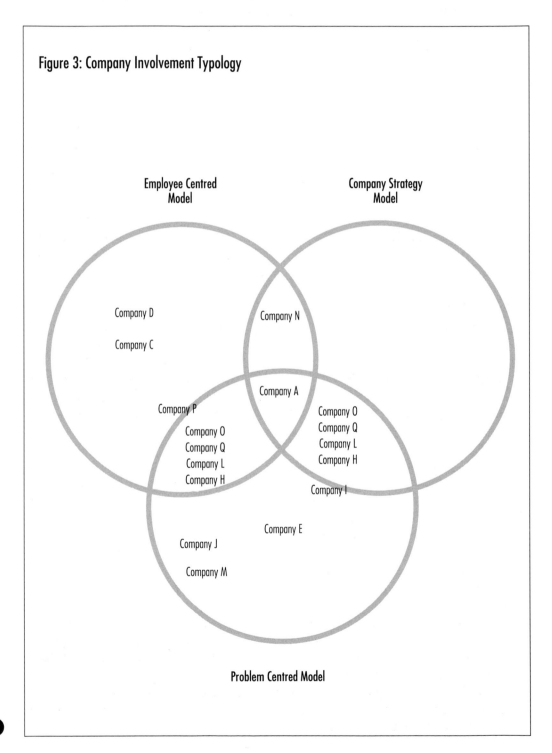

Figure 3: Company Involvement Typology

4.3 A Typology of Company Involvement in Basic Skills Training –
Outline of Key Classifications

Although our typology is based upon an exclusive categorisation, the real world is less tidy, and inevitably some of our case studies fall between classifications, or contain elements of two or more approaches. The key classifications are summarised below.

Employee Centred Model

Certain companies surveyed were actively supporting basic skills training as result of a view amongst senior managers that it was generally "a good thing" that employees should be able to improve their basic skills. Benefits to their performance at work, if perceived at all by managers, were considered secondary and indirect. Thus participation in the programme tends to be voluntary on the part of individuals, who are therefore randomly drawn from different departments and levels. The training programme itself is individual rather than company centred. Training will often lead to some form of formal accreditation where this is regarded by the individual as important added value.

In reality these companies do benefit directly from these programmes in terms of the enhanced skills and confidence of the participants. This fact was perceived by the participants themselves, and by some line managers, but often only to a very limited extent by those senior managers responsible for allocating training resources.

Company Strategy Model

In its idealised form (not directly reflected in any of our case studies) this model describes a company which has adopted a corporate business strategy of which human resource assessment and development is a fully integrated component (the Investors in People Model). The company has identified a deficiency in certain areas of basic skills as a key obstacle preventing workforce progression to more advanced training, or as a factor in production inefficiency and proposes to tackle this deficiency in a planned manner as part of its overall corporate strategy.

The training programme is thus directly tailored to company requirements, and individuals are selected for training by the company based upon an analysis of their individual needs in the context of their developing role within the company. Training may not be formally accredited unless the company sees particular merit in this. This model provides direct and tangible benefits to the company, in two of the case studies it formed a central part of the corporate strategy. Benefits to individuals tend to be reflected in terms of job satisfaction and progression, rather than their life outside work.

Problem Centred Model

In contrast to the previous model, involvement in basic skills training is precipitated as a result of a specific difficulty rather than a planned strategy, and the response is designed to overcome the immediate difficulty. Commonly the difficulty arises because individuals have been placed in positions of responsibility for which they are not fully equipped in terms of basic skills. They have been promoted beyond their immediate capabilities as a result of a lack of prior assessment and training. This results in a mini crisis within the organisation as senior managers are forced to pick up the pieces.

Alternatively the company may be being forced into action as a result of external stimuli. Typical examples are the impending requirement for those involved in the production and handling of food to obtain the food hygiene certificate, or for suppliers in industries such as motor components to work to established customer quality and delivery regimes.

In this model the training programme tends to be designed around the immediate needs of the company and individual, it is not based upon a more comprehensive or strategic approach. Training is normally accredited only if this is an externally imposed requirement. Training programmes tend to be limited in extent, highly specific, and often tacked on to other job specific programmes. Participants tend to be provided with a level of knowledge just sufficient to cope with immediate requirements. The (unforseen) benefits of the training experience may however help to propel the employer towards the company strategy model.

In the following sections we draw upon appropriate case studies to describe the way in which these models tend to operate in practice, and their relative effectiveness in meeting operational and strategic objectives.

4.4 Employee Centred Model

A number of our case study examples fit this model to some degree, however the best examples are provided by Company C and Company D and in the following discussion these are used to illustrate the nature of the approach.

Key Objectives – Reasons for Company Involvement

Both Company C and Company D are large companies which have a long history of training provision: both have dedicated training departments. The impetus for getting involved in such training was not because of perceived skill deficits affecting job performance but rather, the acknowledgement that literacy and numeracy problems did exist and that employees should be encouraged to take up training opportunities in this area for their own benefit. An awareness that some employees did have problems with basic skills had been clear for some time in both organisations, but previous efforts to bring together a viable group for training had been unsuccessful. This failure was a consequence of several factors including the considerable stigma which still attaches to poor basic skills.

Course content and delivery

For both these organisations, the primary vehicle through which basic skills training was delivered was the Wordpower programme. In Company C, a group of employees met together at the same time each week and followed an individualised training programme. At Company D, the range of training was wider and also individually tailored, with participants being given their own workplan to work to with a specific tutor. All participants worked on their programmes in the company's Open Learning Centre and negotiated with one of several tutors, what, when and how they wished to study. At Company D, specific units of competence within the Wordpower award were chosen as suitable topics for study, and most participants were interested in improving particular skills such as oral communication, reading plans, writing reports and so on. As with Company C, the tutors delivering the programme came from outside the organisation and both companies suggested that this was a crucial factor in its success. For both sets of participants, the fact that training was available on site was one of the most important aspects of the programme, because it was convenient, particularly for those without transport to get to college sites, and peer pressure worked to encourage continued involvement. In both organisations, participation in the programme was voluntary and mostly self-directed: only in a couple of instances had suggestions been made by other people that individuals should participate.

Outcomes for individual employees

The outcomes for individuals depended on their reasons for joining the programme in the first place. For many, the establishment of the programme and the general invitation to join, had prompted them to really think about their own skill levels and to decide that they were willing to brave the possible jibes of their colleagues in order to improve their skills. All programme participants saw improvements in basic skills as both ends in themselves and as a way of gaining an extra advantage over possible job competitors.

None believed that a lack of skills made them poor at their jobs, but rather that an improvement would lead to them being more effective and, possibly, being given different tasks to do, with additional responsibilities. For participants at both Company D and Company C, improvements had been made in all the key basic skills areas, with straightforward reading and writing skills being those which had improved most significantly. When asked to make self-assessments of the extent of improvements in self-confidence, communicating with others and handling money, the majority of participants were able to detect positive shifts in these skill areas.

Many participants reported feeling more able to communicate in group situations at work and were more willing to offer opinions: some have also discovered the extent of their colleagues deficiencies in basic skills. Most participants believed that the possession of better basic skills would stand them in good stead for the future, although there was considerable uncertainty about whether improvements in basic skills would necessarily encourage promotion. There was an acknowledgement that every organisation needs employees to work at different levels and that there were very few opportunities for advancement at the lower end of the organisational hierarchy.

Outcomes for the company

Although neither of the two companies had attempted to quantify the benefits of the programme, both sets of managers interviewed reported that intuitively they considered the training to have been a success. Having already suggested that a lack of basic skills had not affected company performance in the past, it would in have been surprising if these companies then reported significant and tangible increases in production efficiency as a result. Line managers did however report less tangible benefits of improved self-confidence, morale, flexibility and team skills, acknowledging that these must affect work performance. There was also a specific acknowledgement that the improved confidence of scheme participants meant that they would be more likely to get involved in group activities such as quality circles and the employee suggestion scheme.

These perceptions of benefits to the company over and above those to individual employees were common at lower and intermediate levels of management, but apparently less common at senior management level. This was evidenced by the reasons reported by training managers for difficulties experienced in securing resources for further provision of this nature.

Interviews with employees showed them to be well aware that the programme provided skills which are personally useful and also essential for the company's future success. For all the participants, improvements in basic skills have led to more confidence so that they are more efficient and effective, their performance is better and therefore the company saves money. If people are not frightened by the written word, then they are more likely to read manuals, notices and so on, and more likely to contribute to, say, the suggestion scheme, and therefore, potentially, save the company money. With improvements in vocabulary and understanding, people will make fewer mistakes through misunderstanding.

Other issues

Some participants experienced problems with colleagues who resented the time off which they received through attending the course. Whilst many line managers had been very supportive of their staff's attendance, colleagues sometimes felt that the situation was unfair. There have also been occasions where participants were prevented from attending because their production unit had to complete an urgent or unexpected order, but this was recognised as entirely legitimate by all programme participants.

4.5 The Company Strategy Model

Seven of our case studies exhibited many of the characteristics of this model, although many had elements of the problem centred approach. In several instances companies had been prompted to think more strategically as a result of some crisis or external threat in the company's recent history.

Company F and Company G provide similar and useful examples of the issues and the approach, particularly so as their circumstances are typical of many small/medium sized manufacturing companies, and because they serve to illustrate a range of positive outcomes which can accrue. Our judgement has been that in relative terms, of the companies in this category the value for money outcomes of the training have proved the most effective in these two examples.

Key Objectives – Reasons for Company Involvement

Both companies had got the message that in order to improve their productive efficiency they needed to consider their utilisation of supervisory level staff on the shop floor. Previously training had been almost wholly directed towards technical and managerial levels. This strategy did not arise through any natural process of enlightenment so much as a result of external threats to the company's survival, coupled with the injection of new ideas.

Company G recognised that it had to increase productivity in order to survive, and that initially at least, new investment was not an option. Their incoming MD recognised the potential contribution that could be made by shop floor supervisors in this process, and the importance of interpersonal and communication skills.

Company F recognised that supplier customer relationships in the intensely competitive motor components sector were changing radically, and that the adoption of production systems and organisational structures pioneered by the Japanese was essential if the company was to survive. Having introduced those structures, the company found that they were not working effectively, the reason being that the team leaders who were expected to play a critical role did not have the basic communication and interpersonal skills which their new responsibilities demanded.

Thus, whilst the company had attempted to act strategically, it found itself veering towards a problem centred approach because it had failed to adequately appraise training needs at the outset. Most importantly however, it did subsequently come to recognise the strategic relevance of basic skills.

Having had virtually no previous experience of basic skills training, or indeed any type of extended formal training for shop floor personnel, both companies embarked upon the project as something of an act of faith, with only partial knowledge of the likely benefits. In both cases the training involved a largely horizontal layer of team leaders/supervisors from production and allied areas such as stores and quality. The compulsory attendance of a relatively large group proportionate to the size of company itself ensured a level of corporate impact in excess of that obtained through the more random employee centred model.

Although arguably at the 'enlightened' end of the spectrum, at the beginning of the project both companies exhibited signs of traditional management/workforce relationships still typical of much of British manufacturing industry. Two-way communication between managers and shop floor workers both horizontally and vertically, was under-developed, as was the involvement of the workforce in production planning. No doubt partly as a result of this, there was evidence of something of a culture of mistrust and conflict and of 'crisis management'.

The Design of the Training

The focus of the training in both cases was communication skills, including such areas as accepting and responding to criticism, holding meetings, presenting opinions, report writing, handling disciplinary issues, being assertive etc. Needs for literacy support varied between employees, and this support was provided as an integrated part of the programmes. The presentation of the course was clearly important, providers considered that the use of the term 'basic skills' would have stigmatised the course and reduced the willingness of employers and employees to participate. The opportunity to hang literacy support on the peg of communication skills was therefore very important.

Key Outcomes

In overall terms it is clear that the high levels of effectiveness of these training programmes stemmed not only from course content, but from the context within which the courses were developed and delivered. The key benefits being:

1. **Initial high level trainee motivation.** Despite ignorance of the nature/purpose of the training – training was previously seen as being for managers only – the provision was seen as an expression that the supervisors were valued; it conferred status.

2. **Communication/peer group support.** Individual employees had previously had little opportunity for extended communication with each other. There were several reasons for this – discrete production cells, noise levels on the shop floor, the shift system, the remote location of stores, design departments etc.

    Supervisors could become isolated as individuals – their role often perceived as a buffer between management demands and workforce grievances. Thus the course provided a forum for shared experiences and problems, reducing isolation. Course pressures/required participation and coursework reinforced the 'bonding' process. This in turn led to a significant mitigation of the conflict culture and a willingness to adopt a constructive/objective approach to resolving cross-departmental issues.

3. **Self – Confidence/Assertiveness.** In both companies it was clear that the lack of these qualities was a significant barrier preventing supervisors/team leaders from contributing their knowledge and experience towards improving company performance. The training clearly had a major beneficial effect in this area, demonstrated by a markedly higher level of employee participation at meetings involving more senior managers.

Taken together all of the above outcomes resulted in an important 'cultural' shift in working relationships on the shop floor, with supervisors/team leaders playing a much more pro-active role in production planning, and assuming a higher level of responsibility and decision taking.

The above benefits were underlined by the highly positive comments of the production managers, neither of whom were particularly enthusiastic about the training at the outset in view of its potential disruption to production.

The employees interviewed were universally enthusiastic about the benefits of the training, subject to some minor niggles. These benefits may be summarised in two ways:

i) **a sense of achievement in having mastered new skills – for many of the participants this was a novel experience**

ii) **increased sense of worth and job satisfaction in the workplace.**

The company strategy approach illustrated by these two examples is fully consistent with current progress towards Total Quality Management and Investors in People. Its importance in this wider context is discussed in the concluding section of this report.

4.6 The Problem Centred Model

Companies may require support for basic skills as a result of having identified a particular problem or difficulty which is having a significant effect upon the efficiency of their operations. Had the company adopted a planned approach to human resource development along the lines of IIP or the *Company Strategy Model*, then the problem should have been anticipated.

Many companies do not have a history of training, particularly SMEs, and tend to get involved in training interventions as a result of external factors, such as the imposition of quality standards by customers (for example Ford's insistence that all its suppliers achieved Ford constructed quality standards) or the requirement to conform to legislation, especially EU law. As we stated in our introduction, inevitably the case studies do not fit the typology perfectly, however probably the most interesting examples of the *Problem Centred Model* are Company I and Company E.

Company I had promoted manual workers to non-manual contract management positions without effective prior assessment of skills and training needs. Consequently problems arose as a result of their inability to cope with the paperwork, terminologies and, to a lesser extent, the interpersonal skill requirements of their new roles. The training was company specific and strongly focused upon reading and writing skills. In terms of outcomes, the training met the (limited) objectives set out very effectively in terms of written skills. Managers also observed 'unforseen' benefits in terms of increased confidence and the ability to communicate more effectively. The success of the course also increased the level of company awareness of the benefits of training more generally.

Company E had established a policy that it wanted all operatives to achieve the *Basic Food Hygiene Certificate,* and had commenced appropriate training programmes. However, there were 12 employees who the company did not feel would be able to achieve the certificate in the time allocated because they lacked sufficient basic skills and all needed English for Speakers of Other Languages (ESOL).

The company recognised that, with the European Single Market and the increasing legislative control exerted by Brussels, it was likely that in the future all catering and other food industries would be required to train their operatives in basic food hygiene skills to a minimum standard. The company contacted the local Environmental Health Officer for advice and it was fortuitous that he knew of the Basic Skills at Work Pilot Programme.

About half the participants emerged from the course with the *Basic Food Hygiene Certificate* and the production director suggested that those individuals who did not achieve certification had more profound ESOL needs than was at first envisaged. For those participants who were interviewed, they were very keen to claim the benefits of training including increased self esteem and confidence and a better knowledge of health and safety issues. It was not clear however, from talking to participants, precisely what technical skills they had learnt, although they did argue that they did their jobs better now because they had more awareness of possible health hazards in a food production environment. The company felt that despite the lack of qualification attainment for some participants, the whole workforce was now better trained and aware and that the company had benefited from its involvement in the programme.

The original aims and objectives of the project were largely achieved, although the poor level of language skills amongst some employees had not been foreseen and some individuals will need a lot more support before they are able, if ever, to achieve a certificate. Most of the work in which participants are involved is mundane and repetitive and does not require high levels of technical ability or literacy/numeracy skills. Low levels of basic skills were therefore easy to overlook since these skills were not required in order to carry out work tasks satisfactorily.

4.7 Conclusions

Whereas most case study examples exhibit characteristics of more than one element of our typology, we nevertheless consider that it represents a valid basis for explaining the varied outcomes of our research. Whereas it is necessary to be cautious about drawing comparisons between programmes of greatly differing size and orientation, we have formed a clear view that, in terms of all round effectiveness, the *Company Strategy Model* has provided the most significant gains in relation to the resources expended. We are also of the view that in this context it is the focus on *communication skills*, with supplementary support in areas of numeracy and literacy, which has provided the most significant benefits.

We have had a limited opportunity to explore the degree to which alternative vocational training programmes cover this ground. Specifically we have studied the various National Examining Board for Supervisory Management (NEBSM) programmes in this context as they appear the most relevant. We have also contacted one or two local centres which provide these courses. Our impression is that whereas these areas are covered to some extent, they do not appear to provide the same depth of experience as in some of our examples, neither are they able to gear the learning to the workplace context in the same way or, of course, provide the related support in basic skills.

5 The Delivery of Basic Skills Support in Workplace Situations – constraints and ways round them

5.1 Introduction

There are clearly a range of potential constraints related to the delivery of basic skills training in work situations. Many are of course common to many training programmes involving production staff. They may be summarised as follows:

(i)   Lack of appropriate accommodation and facilities – e.g. training room.

(ii)   Disruption of production.

(iii)   Interruption by workplace "emergencies".

(iv)   Timing difficulties – because of shiftwork etc.

(v)   Stigma/embarrassment in terms of relationships with work colleagues.

(vi)   The need to design the programme around workplace materials and priorities, and desirability of placing these within an accredited framework of assessments.

(vii)   The costs of delivering the training and the question of who should meet them. Resource problems where small numbers of employees are involved.

In general our experience has been that methods can be found to overcome difficulties given a fundamental willingness on the part of training providers, employees and employers to be reasonably flexible in their approach. By definition our case study research is based upon projects which have been successfully completed. We have no evidence of the number of projects which were stillborn because of these constraints. Our impression from discussions with training providers is that this is unlikely to have been very significant. We have highlighted key areas of difficulty below and have set out a series of possible solutions, although obviously the list is not exhaustive.

5.2 Lack of Facilities

We surveyed two examples of substantial schemes where there was a lack of on-site facilities, in both cases employees were 'bussed' during work-time to a nearby facility. This is obviously the ideal solution provided companies are willing to co-operate, as it ensures full attendance.

The use of mobile facilities is one possible alternative solution. We also highlight in paragraph 5.8 below the appropriateness of off-site training where needs exist across a range of smaller employers.

5.3   Disruption of Production

This is obviously a critical issue where shopfloor workers are concerned, and is clearly an area where compromises often have to be made. All our case study examples had managed to resolve this problem and disruption was at worst minimal. Within the context of the *Employee Centred Model*, the diffuse nature of participation and the existence of permanent factory based learning centres eased the situation significantly. Problems were more significant with the *Company Strategy* and *Problem Centred Models* which often involved release of significant proportions of production workers as a group.

Solutions to the problem were varied, in some instances small groups of workers were withdrawn for training for a short time over an extended period; in others training was provided at the shift interchange, with say an hour of a worker's own time being matched with an hour from company time. Within large companies our experience was that the random release of workers from different cells for short periods was easily accommodated provided colleagues were willing to cover.

In most cases the actual impact on production was considered negligible, being much less pronounced than originally feared in a number of cases. Typically problems were at their worst in the early stages of the training, an initial `shake down' period being required whilst those asked to cover for absent colleagues were learning new responsibilities.

The key to overcoming this difficulty seems to be a willingness to be flexible on all sides, and to make compromises. Thus in at least one instance, the training was extended over a longer period than that ideally recommended in order to minimise the impact on production. Training providers, in particular, clearly need to be flexible in terms of delivery.

5.4   Interruptions

We came across evidence that some projects had found this a problem in the initial stages of training. The problem was overcome in two ways – firstly, there was a natural reduction in the number of shop floor problems as colleagues designated to provide cover came to understand the requirements, and secondly, several employers issued instructions prohibiting interruptions except in extreme emergencies.

5.5   Timing Issues

We have indicated above how shiftwork problems have been addressed. Opportunities also exist to undertake training during maintenance shut down periods, although we came across no examples of this. We identified no major difficulties in this area, however the need for providers to be highly flexible in the hours and dates during which they are prepared to resource the training is clearly paramount.

5.6 Stigma/Embarrassment

This is a difficult issue to which there is no simple solution, although we encountered a number of common elements in positive approaches. The use of the term "basic skills" in marketing the training is not helpful. It clearly has negative connotations for both employers and employees. Most of the programmes we studied were marketed under alternative titles: 'Communication skills' and 'Essential skills' were two examples.

5.7 The Design of Training Programmes – company needs and their relationship to the process of accreditation

Our case study investigations identified two basic approaches to the design of training programmes. In one approach the training programme was designed with accreditation uppermost in mind. Consequently workplace based tasks and materials, sometimes together with non-work related tasks and materials were drawn together to support the achievement of Wordpower or Numberpower. Our experience was that this approach is more common where company needs were expressed in non-specific terms, or where what has been described as the 'employee centred approach' was significant. Examples were Company N, Company C, Company D, and (in the early stages of the project) Company G.

In the second approach the training was designed around specific employer work-related requirements, with accreditation strictly a secondary issue. Once the course had been designed then the issue of accreditation was sometimes considered retrospectively. The programme was subsequently assessed against the Wordpower and Numberpower requirements with appropriate units of competence being accredited.

Both approaches have certain advantages and drawbacks which are dependent upon the context in which the training is delivered. In most cases where accreditation was offered, particularly to the relevant level of Wordpower or Numberpower, this was an important motivating factor for employees, many of whom had never before received a training award. Work-related benefits in these cases were much less specific however i.e. they related more to perceived increases in confidence, motivation and a willingness to put forward ideas, rather than an enhanced ability to perform defined tasks or take on specific responsibilities.

Work-related benefits such as the ability to cope with new organisational structures or responsibilities were obviously far more evident in the second model, together with the less specific benefits outlined above. The range of basic competences achieved was generally narrower however, and thus left the ability of the individual employees to cope with unforseen future changes open to question.

It is clear from the case studies that there is some tension between an approach which is wholly company centred and one which is based upon full accreditation through Wordpower or Numberpower. Sometimes this stems from the provider failing to see how work could be accredited without distortion. Inevitably, some companies have very specific needs which may make the potential for accrediting training limited. Also some employees are motivated by accredited achievements, others are not, and for them the additional work required to achieve full accreditation can be demotivating.

Under these circumstances we consider that formal accreditation should continue to be offered as an option while recognising that it will not always be taken up. This has largely been the case hitherto, although we encountered some understandable pressure from output funded organisations such as TECs and FE Colleges to require that all training be formally accredited.

5.8   Finance

We were not asked to examine the value for money aspects of case study schemes as part of our brief. Additionally, in most cases the relevant information was not available at the level of the individual employer. We do however consider that we can offer some helpful comments on the reported perceptions of companies on the importance of financial assistance as a means of promoting the take up of basic skills training.

The case studies which we examined were financed under the Basic Skills at Work Programme (up to 75% of total cost), with the balance normally being provided by local Training and Enterprise Councils and/or LEAs. Most of the employers we talked to indicated that they would not have proceeded with the training on the scale and/or according to the timetable adopted unless this external financial assistance had been available. In the majority of cases that we examined however the benefits to the company of the training had been perceived by senior management and consequently levels of commitment had been raised. In these cases, where additional training was considered necessary, this was actively being undertaken or planned on the basis that all or a substantial proportion of the costs would be borne by the company. This highlights the importance of "pump priming" finance in promoting the take up of basic skills training.

Projects involving small numbers of employees can obviously be extremely costly to deliver. In three of the examples that we studied there were only one or two employees involved per employer. In one of these the training was delivered off site in an open learning context thereby reducing costs considerably. The others however involved workplace based tutor sessions. Where there is a generic need which encompasses groups of individual small employers, for example food hygiene training combined with ESOL for workers in ethnic restaurants, then there is a clear opportunity to deliver this cost effectively outside the workplace. Some community facilities such as the Dovecote Centre in Northumberland, which has actively supported basic skills at work training, provide facilities for local residents and also cater for the needs of small companies.

6 *Conclusions*

6.1 Introduction

Effectiveness may be assessed at a variety of levels:

(i)   **individual training programmes may be judged in their own terms based upon the objectives set for them by those responsible for their design. These objectives are often very specific and operational in nature**

(ii)   **they may be judged against 'unforseen/unplanned' objectives/benefits/drawbacks**

(iii)   **they may be judged against wider objectives, which are often not made explicit, but may be imputed – for example, their impact upon the wider competitiveness/efficiency of the company/employer**

(iv)   **their impact may be assessed in the wider context of national policies on education and training and the improvement of industrial competitiveness.**

We deal with (i) to (iii) above in the first part of our conclusions (section 6.2 below). The relevance to national policy objectives is dealt with in the second part. Finally we consider a series of practical issues relevant to the design and delivery of programmes which appear to have an important bearing on the effectiveness of the outcomes.

In interpreting our findings we have again drawn upon the typology of company involvement set out in section 4.

6.2 The Effectiveness of Case Studies on an Individual Basis

Within the preceding sections of this report we have summarised and broadly classified the principal outcomes of our research based upon the analysis of the case studies.

In particular we have emphasised the fact that the degree of effectiveness can only be assessed directly by considering the outcomes of the case studies in relation to the varying objectives established for each. These objectives, which were largely inferred from our discussions, stemmed primarily from the very varied perceptions, attitudes and expectations of the relevant companies.

As we have shown in our classification of typologies for company involvement, the nature of these objectives underpinned the form of the design and delivery of the training and hence largely predetermined the nature of the final outcomes.

Our individual case studies (see Appendix 1 and Figure 1 section 4) provide details of our assessed outcomes on a project by project basis. As these show, in the majority of cases, the projects judged on their own terms clearly achieved a high level of effectiveness.

Comparative judgements of relative *cost*-effectiveness are extremely difficult due to the varied nature of the objectives and outcomes. There are also the problems of quantifying outcomes and outputs and identifying and quantifying input costs. Judgements tend therefore, of necessity, to be based upon a synthesis of impressions rather than quantifiable benefits.

These problems are not unique to this research. For the reasons identified there is a general dearth of quantifiable cost effectiveness information in the whole area of company based training provision. Where such information is available it tends to concentrate on the "macro" rather than "micro" level i.e. national or, at best, large company level data based upon training investment across the board rather than the impact of specific programmes.

Turning to specific judgements, we have highlighted two clear cut examples of programmes involving low numbers of employees which by any measure appear very expensive in relation to the outcomes achieved. Additionally there are examples of large company training projects where there has been a significant level of in kind or direct company contributions to programmes (Company C, Company D and Company P, for example). In each of these cases company benefits have been non specific and tangential rather than direct. Thus, in terms of public resources and leverage, the programmes appear efficient, and in terms of specific employee benefits at least, cost-effective.

We would argue however that the most cost effective programmes are those where there are clear and direct benefits to both company and employee. *The Company Strategy Model* provides the best example. Within this context the training makes a clear contribution to corporate survival and growth, whilst at the same time employees are provided with skills which develop their individual potential. As we discuss in the following section, this approach also conforms closely to the philosophy of Total Quality Management and Investors in People – approaches which are now commonly acknowledged as being of critical importance in securing the continued competitiveness of our industrial base.

In terms of benefits largely unforseen by companies and employees at the outset of the programmes, by far the most significant is the almost universal increase in the confidence levels of employees. We suggest that this is due to a variety of factors. In some instances the employees had previously had very little experience of any formal training programmes - consequently the programme represented a tangible sign that they were valued by the company. Some employees reported that they had previously seen training as being `for managers'. Coupled with this, many employees were intimidated by the prospect of being unable to cope with the programme at the outset as a result of negative experiences of school or other training and a poor self-image. Their consequent positive experiences in this respect were undoubtedly a key factor in boosting confidence. We came across no significant unforseen drawbacks to the programmes.

In terms of wider objectives, most programmes had been more effective in boosting company performance than originally anticipated, although company expectations in this area varied greatly in accordance with our typology. In the context of the *Employee Centred Model,* much of this directly derived from the increase in confidence levels referred to above. As a result of this, managers reported an increased willingness to communicate ideas and problems to work colleagues. Improved levels of literacy and numeracy were also clearly important.

Two employers falling within the company strategy typology attributed a quantifiable increase in production output to the training, although there was some uncertainty about the exact level. Two employers at least considered that the training had created a cohesion and flexibility within the workforce which would make it much easier to introduce organisational changes in the future. Several companies reported reduced pressure on production managers as a result of workforce empowerment facilitated by the training programmes.

6.3 The Contribution of Work Based Basic Skills Training to the Achievement of National Targets for Education and Training

In assessing effectiveness it is important not only to consider the extent to which basic skills training can assist in meeting the perceived needs of individual employers and employees, but to consider the contribution that such programmes can make to the achievement of wider objectives. It appears to us that provision of this type has a direct relevance, firstly to the achievement of the National Targets for education and training and secondly in support of wider initiatives directed at improving the competitiveness of UK industry.

The acquisition of basic skills is an essential pre-requisite for attainment of all of the National Targets. Within our typology we suggest that the *Employee Centred* and *Company Strategy Models* offer the greatest contribution towards the achievement of these targets, rather than those programmes which are more narrowly focused. The contribution made by the *Employee Centred Model* – where large firms are involved in terms of providing access to basic skills support for relatively large numbers of individuals – should not be underestimated. Whilst its effectiveness in contributing to company performance may not be as great as the *Company Strategy Model,* it seems to us that it may be regarded as complementary to adult education facilities within the community. Both provide a means of upgrading the basic skills of the population at large. This is particularly important in the light of the fact that about 16% of the adult population suffer from some form of reading or writing difficulty, and that more than half of these are either working or looking for work.

In this context large-company based learning centres offer the following advantages :

- **Easy accessibility for employees who might not be prepared or able to travel from home to access support.**

- **Peer group support/less stigma.**

- **The opportunity to tailor curriculum materials to those commonly in use in the workplace.**

- **Reduced costs as a result of company support.**

Provision of this type does result in demonstrable benefits to the company, both in terms of employee motivation and ability to perform tasks more effectively. However it is not designed with this objective in mind and the evidence suggests that these benefits are not readily perceived by senior management. In part this appears to be because they have a low level of "visibility" – impact is dispersed through the plant because of the way the programme is organised, and quantification of the benefits is very difficult. For the above reasons these programmes can suffer from limited "political" support at senior management level, and are thus inherently vulnerable when budgets are under pressure.

We suggest that provision of this type – which clearly extends beyond basic skills – represents a valuable and cost effective contribution to adult education in the context of the National Targets. In this context it should be actively promoted by a range of agencies – at government level jointly by the Employment Department, DFE and DTI, and at local level by the new integrated regional offices, TECs and LEAs in the context of the new Single Regeneration Budget. Initiatives of this type provide clear opportunities to generate substantial amounts of private sector leverage.

In terms of promotion, clearly this should aim to extend the range of provision of this type amongst larger companies. As part of this process it should also seek to enlighten the senior management of major companies concerning the impact of these programmes on worker morale and effectiveness and company performance.

6.4 The Potential Contribution of Work Based Basic Skills Training in Support of Industrial Competitiveness

British industry is currently in the throes of a profound culture change. This results from the increased importance placed upon the need to increase industrial competitiveness in the face of the advances made by our major partners in the European Union and the rapid emergence of competitor nations from the Pacific Rim. The situation is summarised in the Government's White Paper – 'Competitiveness – helping business to win' – a key part of which relates to the need to increase our level of achievements in the area of education and training. The issues are taken up in the DTI's 'Managing in the 90s' programme, much of which is based upon the concept of Total Quality Management. Key components of this culture change are the linked issues of Quality, Communication Systems, and Work Organisation, and these are the areas highlighted by the IMS in their survey *Basic Skills and Jobs* as being the most common cause of increased demand by companies for basic skills, particularly communication skills.

Moves towards Total Quality Management (TQM) and Investors in People standards also reflect the need to focus on these areas:

❝Total Quality Management implies a top-management led company-wide approach involving all employees and focusing on prevention rather than detection and correction. Customer orientation and teamwork are key features.❞

'The Quality Gurus' – DTI Managing in the '90s series.

As the quotation emphasises, of critical importance in these approaches is the need to involve the **whole workforce** in measures to improve quality and upgrade production efficiency, not just management.

Investors in People is an Employment Department backed initiative which encourages organisations to adopt a planned approach to the training and development of its personnel. It creates a two-way link between an organisation's business strategy and the development of its people. Organisations which achieve the award will have built a total quality framework for the virtuous cycle of commitment, planning, action and evaluation.

British industry unfortunately has to struggle with a tradition of strong demarcation, not to say conflict, between workforce and management, and also horizontally between departments such as design, quality, stores and production. As evidenced in a number of our case studies, changing this culture is not an easy process, and can be intimidating for both workers and management. Central to this is the question of developing the right communication and interpersonal skills amongst key personnel – particularly shop floor supervisors/teamleaders. The ability to de-personalise criticism, to put forward ideas assertively, to understand the position of others, to optimise the outcomes of meetings, to listen, to respect the differences between other people etc. are critical in this process. Other skills – the ability to write reports or memos and to interpret instructions – are important but ancillary.

A number of our case studies have shown in very clear terms, the all round effectiveness of this approach, notably:

- **The motivating effect which the provision of training can have upon sections of the workforce. It is a sad comment on British industry that in many companies training, and particularly training in organisational and communication skills is seen as relevant only to the needs of managers.**

- **The value of being able to share problems and experiences with others in similar positions in a non-confrontational context. The traditional approach is that shop floor discussions are only held when things go wrong, with the attribution of blame being at least as big an issue as finding a solution to the problem.**

- **The direct benefits which arise as a consequence of the training – both to the trainee in terms of increased confidence, responsibility and self- esteem, to the company in terms of increased production efficiency and a more flexible adaptable workforce, and to senior management in terms of their ability to concentrate on strategic rather than crisis management.**

6.5 The Need to Raise Levels of Employer Awareness

There are a series of barriers which remain to be overcome if the approach described above is to take root. Our research has shown that one of the most significant of these is company awareness.

The history of the development of the Pilot Projects through the BSAW programme suggests that participating companies tend to have been drawn largely from those more likely to have had a prior commitment to training, and hence an existing relationship with the local TEC or education providers.

Despite this it is evident from our case studies, that the identification of basic skill needs, and also of the means of addressing those needs, has more often occurred as a result of fortuitous accident or response to a crisis or problem than as a result of a formal process of human resource planning and appraisal linked to corporate strategy. Thus, even within the "more enlightened" population of companies the question of awareness appears to be critical.

Awareness in this context can be broken down into a series of sequential elements as follows:

1. Managers need to be aware of the importance and relevance of basic skills competences amongst staff at all levels as a means of improving competitiveness.

2. Managers need be aware of the extent to which these skills are deficient in their current workforce, and/or the impact that changes in work organisation, quality systems etc. will have on skill requirements in these areas.

3. Having identified these needs, managers need to be aware of the agencies able to offer support for the development of basic skills. Our impression is that this information is not well known: within industry training awareness tends to centre around management development and vocational/ technical support, not support for basic skills.

4. Lastly, recognising the production manager's reaction to any proposals for the provision of training to groups of production staff, there needs to be an awareness that it is perfectly possible for this training to be delivered in non-traditional ways – i.e. at the workplace, at times stipulated by the company, and with minimal disruption to production.

Companies need to surmount all four of the above awareness barriers if basic skills needs are to be properly identified and an appropriate response developed. In this context it is unsurprising that in many of our case studies, action had been precipitated by crisis and/or coincidence.

Turning to the issue of the wider population of companies, there is a substantial amount of indirect evidence to suggest that the employer/employee needs addressed within the *Basic Skills at Work Pilot Programme* represent the tip of a very substantial iceberg. This evidence is based upon the assessed level of basic skills within the workforce at large, the low level of commitment to training generally within UK companies (see section 2 of this report), and the traditional attitude of many companies to the issue of workforce training.

To amplify this latter point, our experience of many traditional manufacturing concerns suggests that typical perceptions at senior management level are that training is primarily only of benefit in assisting managers to manage (ie give instructions to the workforce), and that training for shop floor staff is only relevant if it is of a very specific technical or vocational orientation.

It is clear that addressing these major issues which link fundamentally the concepts of education, training and improving industrial competitiveness requires a multi-agency approach reflecting commitment at the highest level. The fact that they cut across the brief of three different government departments is not helpful, although again the development of integrated offices at the regional level offers an opportunity.

ALBSU cannot hope to tackle these issues alone, indeed as we have indicated, limited progress is being achieved in areas outside those labelled basic skills, for example by organisations involved with the provision of NEBS training which includes similar elements. Our experiences show that attempts to introduce innovative organisational structures such as quality circles and team working are doomed to failure if the individuals concerned are not equipped with the required range of basic skills. It appears to us that there is a frequent tendency to overlook this fact and it is very important that awareness in this area is increased – not just amongst companies, but amongst those advising and assisting them in achieving "world class" standards.

It is our firm view that the issues and needs identified in this report will be readily recognised and supported by those concerned to assist companies to come to grips with these standards, within which we consider the role of initiatives such as Total Quality Management and Investors in People to be central.

6.6 Developing and Delivering Work Based Basic Skills Training – Maximising Effectiveness

In this final section of our conclusions we highlight a series of practical issues derived from our examination of case studies which we feel can help maximise the positive outcomes of programmes.

Our case studies show a wide range of variation in the degree to which programmes were tailored to company needs. In the case of the *Employee Centred Model* this issue is less relevant. However in the other models it is a central issue of direct relevance to the effectiveness of the training.

We suggest that a tailored programme needs to take into account the following factors:

1. The need to clearly establish a shared vision of the training with the company. Specifically this means setting out the objectives of the training within the context of (a) the copmany's corporate strategy; (b) any specific issues or problems which the training is intended to resolve.

    Some companies will have a narrow view of the contribution which basic skills training can make to the efficiency of their company. Others are likely to be unaware of the extent of training needs within their workforce. These problems can often be successfully addressed through audits of training needs. If the company has an awareness of and empathy with the TQM approach then these audits can be extended into 'corporate culture and attitude surveys' (see for example: 'Managing the Total Quality Transformation' – Berry 1991).

2. The need to involve all the relevant company personnel in developing the specification for the training and in the design process. In one of our examples the initial exclusion of the production manager led to some hostility and early difficulties.

3. The need to achieve a balance in the delivery of the training between the need to minimise disruption to production, and the need to mount a well targeted and cost effective training programme.

4. The need to recognise that formal accreditation of the programme will place significant extra demands on the employees and the company – therefore this should not be imposed, but should be incorporated only if there is clear support for it from both parties.

5. The need to carefully develop the programme around company materials and procedures in fairly common use or shortly to be adopted, in order to ensure its relevance.

6. The need to market the provision very carefully from the earliest stages. The terminology 'Basic Skills' should be avoided in view of its obvious stigma. Numeracy and literacy support should be provided as part of a wider programme of training, rather than in the form of discrete one off provision.

7. The need to bear in mind the importance of broader communication skills, and to ensure that needs in this area are fully assessed.

8. The need to conduct some form of prior assessment of employees on an individual basis prior to the design phase in order to assess not only their competences, but also the particular nature of the challenges they face at the workplace, particularly if their role has changed or is about to.

Many of these issues will appear obvious to those involved with these programmes on a regular basis. We believe however that it is important to flag these up for the benefit of those sponsoring the training and those who may be becoming involved in training in the workplace for the first time.

In order to fully take into account the above issues, we consider that it is most important that the appropriate tutor(s) have a basic empathy with the operating environment of the client company. This implies prior experience of working in a manufacturing or service industry environment as appropriate.

We believe that the lessons learnt from our research have a relevance to a wide range of organisations – Government Departments, Industrial Organisations, Training and Enterprise Councils, Education and Training providers and all those concerned with the provision of business and training advice and resources.

Part 2

Case Studies Arising from the Research

Contents

Company G

The Context – Background to the Company and how the Training Need was Identified

Company G manufactures sophisticated audio equipment. The production process consists of assembling electronic components onto bought in PC boards and assembling the boards themselves onto a frame. The process is only partially automated, with much hand soldering and component selection. A range of different products are being assembled at any one time and production schedules can vary on a daily basis. The firm employs 70 people, including around 50 operatives and 12 supervisors, plus technical, managerial and administrative staff. The company was in great difficulty 4 years ago, with liquidation in prospect, when it was taken over by a larger foreign owned group. Following the takeover a new MD was appointed.

The company recognised that it had to take a hard look at itself if it was to survive. Production volumes had to be increased, quality had to be improved, and yet there was little money for new investment. A DTI sponsored report had stated that the company was overly orientated towards production rather than quality. It pointed to the need to review the role of the supervisors, who at that time were 100% orientated towards production, and to the need to enhance their level of responsibility. The company recognised this as a weakness, noting that supervisors from different departments hardly ever spoke to one another, and that there was little team working.

A chance contact with a local Basic Skills provider arose because the latter were seeking work placements for unemployed people. Discussions led to the identification of the provider as possible deliverer of training based upon communication skills, and to the identification of resources via the TEC and ALBSU. It was therefore decided that a course should be provided for the 12 supervisors. One third of the participants were women and two thirds men. Ages ranged from twenties to late fifties.

The Design of the Course

The course was designed following meetings with workers and management in order to meet their identified needs, which centred on communication and interpersonal skills, but with some help on understanding written instructions and writing reports and memos. Subsequently, following pressure from the TEC, elements of the course were identified which could be accredited under Wordpower. Although not designed around company specific elements and materials, slots were allocated in the sessions for people to bring in and discuss work related material.

There was a fairly common core of works procedures: forms/grids, reference systems, manuals, memos, logs etc. An intimate knowledge of Wordpower was required in order to understand where each slotted in. Significantly, whereas the Training/Quality Manager was closely involved in the initial design of the course, the Production Manager was not.

As the course got under way, the design was adapted firstly as a result of concerns expressed by the production manager, which centred around his perception that the participants were becoming more assertive/argumentative. (He subsequently became very supportive of the course – see Evaluation.) Secondly, the course was changed to reflect the fact that participants began bringing in company forms and instructions, either because they required help with them, or because they represented evidence of achievement.

The Delivery of the Course

Delivery was heavily constrained by the need to maintain production. At the company's request the employees were divided into two groups of six who spent 3hrs training on alternate Mondays. Each group spent 10 weeks in training, a total of 30hrs, over a period of 20 weeks. The course commenced on 1st November and was completed on 18th April. A supplementary module was held in May to assist with putting portfolios together.

Because of lack of facilities in the company the course was delivered at the a local basic education centre, a ten minute car journey away. The supervisors reported for work at 8.00am as usual, attended to any pressing production issues for the day, and then left to attend the course between 9.00am and 12 noon. The fact that the training was remote from the workplace was seen as a positive advantage by both employees and managers. Reasons were freedom from interruptions and that it gave the course a special kudos. Attendance was almost 100%.

OUTCOMES

Accredited Outcomes

At the time of our survey it was expected that all but two employees would achieve Wordpower Level 2. The qualification was optional, and involved additional work in their own time, and one or two participants were less enthusiastic about this.

47

The Impact on the Participant

Discussions were held with a random sample of 6 participants. Most had little knowledge of the course content, or expectations of the course when it first started. All were extremely positive about the benefits of the course. Key benefits reported by all respondents were:

- **An increase in confidence, particularly in giving opinions and expressing ideas.**

- **A closer working relationship with colleagues and less reticence in communicating with managers.**

- **The opportunity of getting together with other supervisors meant that they were able to understand each others difficulties, which had resulted in a much greater degree of teamworking.**

Respondents required to write memos or reports considered they had more confidence in doing so, although for most this was not relevant. Most participants valued the chance to obtain a qualification, and considered this an important plus factor, even though they complained about the amount of their own time they had to spend on homework, and of some difficulties in identifying appropriate evidence for portfolios.

The only significant criticism of the course was that it was drawn out over too long a period of time. With fortnightly intervals between sessions it was difficult to remember what had gone before. This arose as a result of the need to minimise disruption to production. All participants considered that the company had benefitted from the course as a result of increased teamworking, and increased production as a result.

The Training Manager noted:

> ❝The confidence levels of the supervisors shot up. They were quite happy to stand up and talk about themselves, whereas previously they were very quiet and would say nothing at meetings. It has all changed❞.

The Impact on the Company

Initially the course had caused some disruption to production and the Production Manager had to step in to deal with some problems which would otherwise have been dealt with by absent supervisors. After the first few weeks these problems disappeared as supervisors spent more time pre-planning the days production prior to attending the course, and as other supervisors/operatives designated to cover became conversant with what was required of them.

The Production Manager commented that previously the company lacked a good team of supervisors:

❝I spent all my time telling people what to do❞.

He had not become involved in the initial design of the course, and in the early stages became alarmed as he noticed that the supervisors were becoming more assertive and argumentative. As a consequence he then became more involved in the development, particularly team working aspects and his view of the course became much more positive. His comments when interviewed towards the end of the course were as follows:

❝We now have a good team who are working well together❞.

❝They are starting to think ahead – to plan❞.

❝They recognise that they have responsibilities and are confident in handling them, as a consequence I am able to pass on more responsibility❞.

Over the period of the course the average value of daily production throughput increased by about 45%. The Training Manager attributed this to the benefits of the course. The Production Manager's view was that this would have been achieved anyway (because they had to do this to survive), however the basic skills training had enabled it to be achieved more easily. A situation now existed where further production increases would be readily achievable. The Managing Director who had been instrumental in initiating the training was equally enthusiastic about its benefits.

As a result of the course the company had introduced a system of morning team meetings to plan the day's production, involving all departments which was working very successfully. Previously this activity had been tried and failed. The company management had also asked for a course to be designed and provided for their benefit to enable them to communicate more effectively with the workforce, and to identify basic skill needs.

Company F

The Company

Company F manufactures rubber extrusions for the automotive industry, many of them for export. The process requires tight quality control.

Many shopfloor workers are highly skilled, and the company considers it essential to involve them to help resolve quality or technical problems when they occur. The company employs 370 staff having been established on a new site four years ago, with a locally recruited workforce. It is expanding.

How the Need was Identified

The company recognises that it must pursue world class standards if it is to survive and expand. It was therefore in the process of introducing Japanese style organisational systems – specifically, quality circles, cell working with team leaders, and a factory PA system which team leaders were expected to use to announce their achievements.

Having recently promoted and recruited a number of people as part of this new approach, the company was experiencing difficulties in putting it into practice. The newly promoted team leaders were intimidated by quality meetings and, therefore, not contributing to them. Also a range of individuals were unable to cope with the paperwork required because of literacy problems.

The solution to the problem was discovered largely by accident. The Training Manager was attending evening classes at an FE College and had contact with the College's basic skills unit. During discussions he recognised the relevance of their support to the company situation. The availability of funding under the BSAW Programme helped him to sell the idea to other managers.

The Employees Involved

Those selected for the course were individuals recently promoted to team leader status (in effect working supervisors), together with two recently promoted engineers who in their new roles were having to cope with writing reports and issuing written instructions. There were eight employees in all, three women and five men, encompassing a wide age range. An earlier training needs analysis had helped in identifying people needing support. One or two of the supervisory level employees were already doing NEBSM courses.

The issues to be Tackled

The Training Manager identified a number of issues. Communication difficulties occurred because instructions used excessive technical jargon which could not be understood by operators; the numberwork required in Statistical Process Control needed to be simplified and demystified; people seemed reluctant to commit themselves to paper and were embarrassed by their lack of basic skills; and newly promoted Team Leaders were self conscious in contributing to meetings.

The Design of the Training

The overall theme of the training was "Communication and Report Writing". Management and shopfloor personnel were consulted in the design. The main issue raised by the latter were the difficulties of communicating with their peers.

The course was directly tailored to company needs and individual strengths and weaknesses. Key aspects of the course were assertiveness, negotiating and de-personalising criticism. The course was based on company procedures and documentation, concentrating on those which were in common use – e.g. disciplinary procedures. The course was not formally accredited. Managers and employees interviewed perceived no particular advantage in this.

The course totalled 16 hours per trainee in eight modules of 2 hours, with one two hour session per week involving all employees. The training was held at the time of the shift interchange with employees undertaking one hour in their own time and one in the employers time. The training was held in an on-site training room. Interruptions were not a significant problem.

The Impact of the Training upon the Employees

A key benefit for the team leaders involved was an increase in their rapport with fellow workers. In the shopfloor situation they had very little opportunity to communicate with workers in other cells or on other shifts. This improved rapport resulted in increased confidence through sharing problems and experiences and some specific improvements to production organisation and efficiency. Other key benefits were greater confidence in communicating with managers and in putting forward opinions and ideas, and an increased ability to cope with new responsibilities.

Mixing individuals from the engineering and production sides resulted in much more positive relationships as a result of enhanced understanding of each others' problems and constraints. As a result subsequent discussions around quality issues were much more positive and constructive.

A common impression gained from the employees was that they were 'hungry' for more training. Their criticisms of the course were that particular areas might have been covered in more depth, although these varied with the individual. Those involved with NEBSM courses commented that there was some overlap, but nevertheless were equally enthusiastic about the benefits. One of the employees, previously a setter promoted to a supervisory position, had subsequently written an article for the company magazine. His manager stated "there is no way that he would have achieved this previously".

Typical comments were:

‘I am now more confident all round’.

‘It helped relationships between the engineering and production sides, there is more of a mutual understanding of problems’.

‘I was very afraid of the "Karaoke" (factory PA system), but I am now able to cope with it’.

Overall the benefits of the oral communication aspects appeared much more apparent than the written side. This was partly because most of the employees interviewed stated that they felt they already had these skills or did not need them in their work situation. They may however require them in the future.

Impact on Company Performance

The Training and Production Managers commented upon the "visible increase in confidence" of the employees, the fact that they appeared to "give more thought to quality". Other comments were that the individuals participated far more at team meetings, being "willing to say their piece", and not afraid to speak in front of an audience. Managers also observed an increase in the ability to de-personalise criticism, and a reduction in the tendency to automatically take an adversarial stance. As a result of this there was a clear view that productive efficiency had improved and that teamworking and quality control were also more effective. The company was unable to measure this in quantitative terms however.

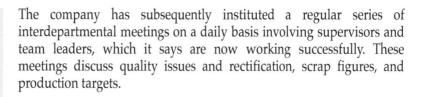

The company has subsequently instituted a regular series of interdepartmental meetings on a daily basis involving supervisors and team leaders, which it says are now working successfully. These meetings discuss quality issues and rectification, scrap figures, and production targets.

Disruption to production caused by the training was described as negligible.

Company C and Company D

Company context/reasons for involvement

Both Company C and Company D are large companies in the automotive sector which have a long history of training provision. Both have dedicated training departments. The management style of both these companies could be loosely described as employee centred, as far as basic skills training is concerned. The impetus for getting involved in such training was not because of perceived skills deficits affecting job performance but rather the acknowledgement that literacy and numeracy problems did exist and that employees should be encouraged to take up training opportunities in this area for their own benefit. At Company C, for example, an awareness that some employees had problems with basic skills had existed for some time, but previous efforts to bring together a viable group for training had been unsuccessful. The training manager believes that this failure was a consequence of the considerable stigma which still attaches to poor basic skills and argues that individuals have much less fear about articulating problems with number skills. For Company C then, the BSAW programme provided a means by which to re-establish efforts to provide literacy training without having to fund such a programme from its own continuing education and training (CET) budget. In the context of voluntary participation and a limited budget for nonwork related CET, there is a perpetual tension between the training needs identified by trainers and those perceived by the workforce.

Company D's participation in the BSAW programme was encouraged by the local College and the company's reasons for involvement were broadly similar to those of Company C in that the programme was seen as being primarily beneficial to individuals rather than the organisation. As well as offering basic skills training in the workplace, the Company D programme extended to two other sites in the local community, with the specific aim of benefiting individuals in those communities. There was also a view, similar to Company C, that although current recruitment and selection processes would screen out individuals with low levels of basic skills, a proportion of older, more established members of the workforce were poorly skilled and would benefit from upskilling. As with Company C, the company had tried to tease out the extent of poor skills through running taster courses, but take-up was minimal.

Course content and delivery

For both these organisations, the primary vehicle through which basic skills training was delivered was a programme built round the Wordpower certificate. In Company C, a group of employees met together at the same time each week and followed an individualised training programme. Assessments of skill levels were made of each participant and they were started off at different points in the Wordpower framework. They would often be engaged in the same type of task, for example, report writing, but expected to demonstrate different levels of skill complexity. At Company D, the range of training was wider and also individually tailored, with participants being given their own workplan to work to with a specific tutor and deciding when they would like to study. All participants worked on their programmes in the company's Open Learning Centre and negotiated with one of several tutors, what, when and how they wished to study. At Company D, specific units of competence within the Wordpower programme were chosen as suitable topics for study, and most participants were interested in improving particular skills such as communication, reading plans, writing reports and so on.

As with Company C, the tutors delivering the BSAW programme came from outside the organisation and both companies suggested that this was a crucial factor in the success of the programme. There are several reasons given for this. The first concerns confidentiality. The fact that tutors are not part of the organisation and will not, therefore, pass on any information about poor skills amongst employees, is very important to participants. Second, many employees have had bad experiences of in-house training programmes and again were more sympathetic to a training programme which was seen as outside the organisational framework. For both sets of participants, the fact that training was available on site was one of the most important aspects of the programme. It was convenient, particularly for those without transport, to get to college sites, and peer pressure worked to encourage continued involvement. Interestingly, trainers at Company D insisted that a more organised programme (such as that delivered at Company C) could not work within a manufacturing context because of the imperatives of getting orders out. But the success of the Company C programme provides evidence that regularly organised training sessions can work in industrial settings. In both organisations, participation in the programme was voluntary and mostly self directed. Only in a couple of instances had suggestions been made by other people that individuals should participate.

Outcomes for individuals

The outcomes for individuals depended on their reasons for joining the programme in the first place. For many, the establishment of the programme and the general invitation to join, had prompted them to really think about their own skill levels and to decide that they were willing to brave the possible jibes of their colleagues in order to improve themselves. Many participants report that initially, colleagues had made derogatory comments although part of the reason appeared to stem from worries about their own limitations. Over time, such colleagues became aware of precisely how participants' skills had improved and sometimes, in the case of Company D, joined the scheme belatedly. All programme participants saw improvements in basic skills as both ends in themselves and as a way of giving themselves an extra advantage over possible job competititors. None believed that a lack of skills made them poor at their jobs, but rather that an improvement would lead to their being more effective and, possibly, being given different tasks to do, with additional responsibilities. For participants at both Company D and Company C, improvements had been made in all the key basic skills areas, with straightforward reading and writing skills being those which had improved most significantly. When asked to make self assessments of the extent of improvements in self confidence, communicating with others, and handling money, the majority of participants were able to detect positive shifts in these skill areas. Many participants reported feeling more able to communicate in group situations at work and were more willing to proffer opinions: some have also discovered the extent of their colleagues' deficiencies in basic skills.

❛We were all talking and this bloke came up and wanted to spell a word and he (a fellow programme participant) just spelt it straight off and the bloke stood there gobsmacked❜.

❛I didn't realise how many people on the factory floor can't spell. I always thought it was only me but I can pick it up better now❜.

❛In my job I have to write out the shiftboards, between the shifts, and since doing it (the course) my spelling has improved, as has my grammar and layout. I think about what I'm going to write now, and how I'm going to put it down. Before I used to just bung it down on a bit of paper. It makes me stop and think about what message I'm trying to convey to other people❜.

❛With the kids, I find that I don't have to ask them how to spell things so often. My youngest daughter has started to encourage me by buying books. My wife won't help me with my spelling, she says I can look it up for myself❜.

❛Before I was quite confident about spelling but got it wrong but now I think, that doesn't look right. I plan things out now❜.

‘Before, if I had to write anything I just wouldn't bother writing it: I'd get my mum to do it for me. But now I sit down, plan it out and write it myself. I'm much more confident’.

Although most programme participants had the support of their families, women were much more likely to encounter hostility as their confidence levels improved. Some individuals participating in programmes had kept their poor skill levels a secret even from their families and most reported changes in the way in which they feel about themselves and people around them.

‘I've got more respect for myself now. My husband used to all the writing so I didn't have to bother. Now I can do it for myself and I do do it. He used to query my spelling but now he doesn't bother me so much. He's worried that I'm getting better than him and that makes me more determined to do it. It's something now that I've got and no one can take it away from me. When he used to take me apart, I wouldn't bother, but now I can do it for myself, I can get a dictionary and check spellings’.

Improvements in communication skills have also been a very important outcome of participation, both at work and at home. 'Terry' reports that his vocabulary has improved since being on the programme and that his wife and family say that he is now much more assertive in his dealings with them. He suggests that before the programme, his wife always used to write all the letters and he often felt 'feeble' now though, he can do this for himself, with a little help, and he feels he is making more of a contribution to the family.

'Bill' reported that he is much more outgoing now and able to offer opinions, whereas before he would never speak up, even if he knew what was being said was wrong. He has to attend quite a few meetings and he has always sat at the back without saying anything. He was also very anxious about having to write things on flip charts or white boards. Since being on the programme and being given specific support in writing things for other people, he is much more confident in both his verbal and written skills and has no problem in standing up in front of often quite senior colleagues, and making a presentation. Whereas before, he would gather information and arrange it and then give it to someone else to write, thus never being credited, he is now able to write up his own reports and see through tasks from beginning to end. He has also been given additional responsibility from his line manager and although he feels a bit daunted by it all, is confident that he can make a success of his new tasks. 'Jim' is one of the few 'hourly paid' employees in his section most of the others are 'staff' and he now feels that he is their equal and that many people are extremely surprised to find that he is an 'hourly paid' employee. He gets a lot of satisfaction from confounding people's expectations.

'Jenny' had only been attending for a few months but was already seeing some improvements. She reported that she had been talking with a colleague when the other person asked about the spelling of 'personnel'. Jenny was able to offer the correct spelling to her colleague because she had been doing some work on this spelling the week before and she not only felt a huge sense of satisfaction, but also that her colleague looked at her with a new respect. It also made her realise that her perception that everyone else knows everything and that she is the only ignorant person, is completely misplaced and that many people have problems with spelling, even people who she believes are "very intelligent". Jenny had successfully managed to avoid doing much writing: she would always draft something out and then ask a secretary to actually do the writing, which she would then check. She admits to having been (and still is) devious in her strategies for writing avoidance and believes that although she is making improvements, it will be a very long time before she feels she will be capable of writing a letter or report on her own.

'Simon' reported being able to help his children with their homework now, occasionally being able to spell a difficult word with them. He also has more confidence and has "come out of his shell" more since being on the programme. He now finds that learning about grammar and spelling is beginning to make sense to him.

Participating in basic skills training has had the additional effect of raising awareness of the written word more generally. A number of participants reporting being more aware and taking more notice of writing since attending the course and were more likely to read signs and notices in the workplace. This new awareness also applied to social contexts, reading newspapers and so on and many felt that they now read and take in information fully, rather than just getting the barest bones.

❝When I read now, I look at what it's all about. Before I used to just read it but not take it in. Not ask any questions about it, not think what it meant. But now I look at it and think, does that mean what I think it means❞.

❝I read newspapers and understand them more now❞.

❝In the library, with all the notices, I just used to ignore them. But now I'll go and have a look or ask one of the ladies if they've got a certain book, or I'll look it up myself and order it myself. Before I used to go straight to the enquiry desk❞.

Most participants believed that the possession of better basic skills would stand them in good stead for the future, although there was considerable uncertainty about whether improvements in basic skills would necessarily encourage promotion. There was an acknowledgement that every organisation needs employees to work at different levels and that there were very few opportunities for advancement at the lower end of the organisational hierarchy.

Although all the participants and trainers who took part in this study were very positive about the provision of basic skills training, there was a reluctance on the part of some personnel within the two organisations, to support basic skills training for a number of reasons. One seems to be the perception that by upskilling individuals, expectations are increased which then have nowhere to go; the classic antitraining position. Second, is the view that no one in the company actually has basic skills needs which the company needs to address, since the level of skill which most people have is sufficient for them to do their job effectively. The subtext of this argument is that there will always be a requirement for low achievers to work in lowgrade jobs (which has already been recognised by employees themselves), and that if those lacking basic skills are subsequently upskilled, then they will no longer be prepared to do the mundane and routine tasks which are essential to the business. Moreover, they might demand more money. However, one of the trainers argued that this is rarely the case with the kinds of learners who have basic skills needs.

❝Basic skills are transferable and it doesn't necessarily follow that because you have increased your own skill base that you want to aim for the moon. It doesn't work like that. A lot of people are quite happy just doing the job. They don't want anything else. They don't want to be the managing director. They want to get their wage packet and go home❞.

Individuals who had experienced changes in their working practices tended to be those in job areas where a sympathetic line manager recognised improvements in confidence and skills, if not necessarily in performance, and encouraged such individuals to take on more responsibility. Newly acquired confidence in themselves and their skills also led to some participants reporting their willingness to apply for jobs which they would not have done otherwise.

Outcomes for the company

Participants were under no illusions that their companies were taking part in the programme and allowing time off for attendance simply as a generous offer on their part. The workforce at Company C, for example, has been reduced to a third of its original size and it is important that each employee who remains is flexible enough to do a range of activities. One employee told of a time recently when the company, having made significant redundancies, then tried to recruit skilled labour and found that it wasn't available. The company then realised that the workforce they wanted was already employed with them, but that they needed to release latent potential through training and development. Employees are only too well aware that the programme provides skills which are personally useful but also essential for the company's future success.

‘Work practices have changed a lot. You used to tool one machine up and do what you're told but now you've got to be able to go and find out, look for yourself, have control over what you're doing and all this (the programme) helps’.

‘Improving and updating people's skills has proved to be a tremendous advantage to the company. They don't want to employ any more people’.

‘Documentation is becoming more and more important and it's got to the position where we've got to get more involved’.

'Terry' reports that he now does his job by himself whereas before, he always had to get someone else to write up reports for him. Therefore, he is saving the company a considerable amount of money in terms of human resource allocation and efficiency. For all the participants, improvements in basic skills have led to more confidence. If people are not frightened by the written word, then they are more likely to read manuals, notices and so on, and more likely to contribute to, say, the suggestion scheme, and therefore potentially save the company money. With improvements in vocabulary and understanding, people will make fewer mistakes through misunderstanding.

As far as company perceptions are concerned, there was a specific acknowledgement that the improved confidence of scheme participants meant that they would be likely to get involved in group activities such as quality circles and to contribute to group discussions. Commenting specifically on company benefits, one trainer reported that a key gain was improved employee versatility and an increase in the extent to which individuals were willing to participate in the full life of the organisation, including quality groups and the suggestion scheme.

❝People can be fully involved with the business. There's a two way benefit: satisfaction to the individual in a much richer working life but that individual has a great deal to contribute in terms of experience and knowledge that the company can draw on when looking at continuous improvement❞.

One line manager commented that the more employees are given the skills to make inputs into the production side, the more the company will benefit. Companies are beginning to realise that the people who work on the shop floor are precisely those who are best placed to know when things could be organised better, planned better, when jobs could be done more efficiently and so on. If employees work in the sort of environment where their views are valued, then they are more likely to take pride in what they do and more likely to speak up. A more involved and creative workforce must benefit the company. Company D's suggestion scheme is thought to save the company £2m each year. It saves £16m each year from improvements suggested by the quality action groups.

Although neither organisation has attempted to quantify the benefits of the programme, both report the success of the scheme at an intuitive level. Having already suggested that a lack of basic skills had not affected company performance in the past, it would in any case be surprising if these companies then reported significant increases in production. What they do report are the less tangible benefits of improved self confidence, morale, flexibility and team skills.

❝If you take our process improvements, for example, they have quantifiable outcomes, particularly if they are focused around the improvement of a process where a problem has existed and you can then monitor the costs savings. If an individual becomes eligible, by way of this (BSAW) programme, to join in with one of our groups and to work more effectively within that group, you can say that there is a real cash benefit at the end of the day. But as far as other costs are concerned, it is difficult to pin down their relationship with basic skills❞.

One line manager who had two staff involved in the programme reported that the personal confidence of both men has improved dramatically. One participant who had always undervalued himself is now much more confident in his dealing with work colleagues and with the line manager. This confidence has inspired his line manager to give him more complex (and interesting) tasks and in the regular team briefings, 'Joe' has been given project responsibilities which would not have happened prior to the training. 'Joe' is also carrying out a project as part of his training programme which will benefit both the line manager and the company. He is devising a process manual for one of the machines which he works on. 'Dave' was less lacking in oral confidence from the beginning, but was not very good at putting ideas and concepts down on paper. He now has good writing skills and is a more reflective and thoughtful employee, working things out beforehand rather than rushing in with the first idea he has. Both men are now given a more complex array of tasks to complete and they both value this additional responsibility. Both have improved their communication skills as a result of being more confident with language and literacy.

Unexpected issues

Some participants experienced problems with colleagues who resented the time off which they received through attending the course. Whilst many line managers had been very supportive of their staff's attendance, colleagues sometimes felt that the situation was unfair. Some participants do their homework in quiet times on the factory floor and report close interest in their activities by their colleagues. There have also been occasions where participants were prevented from attending because their production unit had to complete an order, but this was recognised as entirely legitimate by all programme participants. Overall, participants, line managers and trainers were very enthusiastic about the positive benefits of scheme participation and were hoping to continue a similar training programme into the future.

Company N

Employer Context

Company N is a privately owned residential nursing home for the elderly employing 82 staff in total at the premises surveyed. It is an accredited *Investor in People* company.

How need came to be identified

The process of identification of a training need was initiated by the training provider who drew the employer's attention to the resources available under the BSAW Pilot. Being an Investor in People, the company funds a lot of training which is usually work-related such as health and safety training. Basic skills training would normally be a low priority. If it had not been for the Pilot it is probable that the training would not have taken place or at least would not have involved so many staff.

Previous experience had shown the company that training of any kind tends to boost the self-confidence of participants and to boost overall staff morale, therefore the management were keen to participate in the BSAW project. The company is aware of the costs associated with not training staff but would not be able to quantify the costs related to a lack of basic skills.

The employees involved

The workforce is predominantly female, many of whom are the main family breadwinners in an area of very high male unemployment. The work is low paid and although semi-skilled carries a great deal of responsibility for the well being of the client.

Because of a culture of training, plenty of staff put their names forward from all functions in the company. (2 domestic staff, 2 kitchen staff, 3 qualified nurses, the deputy matron, the admin' officer, 19 care assistants).

Difficulties experienced by the company and individuals before training took place

In general, the organisation was not experiencing any major difficulties with the competence of the staff before the BSAW project. However, it was hoped that the training would help provide a foundation for other training and staff development. More specifically, it was hoped that participants amongst the care assistants would be better able to write reports and understand written instructions. In the longer term the company also hopes that training will make the workforce more flexible.

Many of the participants had no formal qualifications with a very negative past experience of education. This had produced low self-esteem and an unenthusiastic attitude towards personal development and training amongst a number of the staff.

The design of training

A local training provider was chosen as the training provider because they had made the initial contact and were well known to the company. In order to make the training as accessible as possible the programme was run in-house. This was particularly important for those staff who worked shifts. Notices were placed around the workplace inviting participants. Because of the strong culture of training in the organisation staff readily put themselves forward.

Two one and a half blocks were offered each week to facilitate shift working. Staff could attend either time to suit. Delivery was flexible and individuals could stay for a full hours tuition in a small group or just pick up assignments to take away. The take up amongst staff was very widespread. The Deputy Matron took a conversion course for SEN to RGN. The administration officer undertook NVQ level 3 in business administration and received support for the writing up of evidence. Most of the care assistants are followed the NVQ 2 in caring.

The impact which the training had on individuals' performance at work and the aggregate impact on company performance

The personal benefits to the individuals involved probably exceed the immediate direct benefits to the company. Greater competence with literacy and communication skills has led to greater ability to deal with domestic paperwork such as bills and forms. The scheme noticeably improved the self-confidence of participants. All interviewees felt that they were more self-confident after participating in the scheme. They felt more at ease with dealing with superiors and professional people – in particular social security. Forms were less intimidating. One interviewee had overcome her fear of using the telephone; another said that it had got her brain ticking over again.

Managers found it very difficult to assess the contribution to the firm's performance particularly in cash terms. The perception was that greater awareness of the costs of equipment will lead to some savings for the company. The Deputy Matron felt that since the beginning of the scheme, communication was clearer, report writing on clients had improved and the general atmosphere was happier.

Unforeseen benefits/ drawbacks of the training

The Matron was very surprised at the level of response and this has made her more aware of this type of need. She is training manager for the group of companies and as a result of the success of the BSAW project she is raising awareness at head office level and the other sites run by the company.

Practical issues of delivery

Although a large proportion of staff (about one third of the workforce) and particularly of the care assistants were involved in the scheme, disruption of the service was minimal. Contact time was at a shift changeover. Half an hour of work's time is allowed for the participants but many of the staff attended in their own time, even during leave periods.

Costs

The company is aware of the costs associated with not training staff but would not be able to quantify the costs related to a lack of basic skills. Specifically, the costs of the BSAW project have been virtually nil. Theoretically the company lost half an hour's work for each participating employee each week of the training. In practice the staff covered for each other so that the company did not have any problems maintaining the service to clients and did not have to pay extra to those undertaking cover duties.

Overall comments on usefulness and effectiveness

Overall this project would appear to have given a very effective use of resources. In total, 28 members of staff participated on a drop-in type basis during the weekly visits from the tutor. From the company's and individuals' points of view the delivery of training on-site minimised disruption and virtually eliminated the costs to the organisation.

The usefulness of the basic skills training to the organisation has already become apparent in terms of improved communication and written skills. In the longer term it is likely that the basic skills training will have provided a firm base for other forms of training and staff development.

The benefit for individuals has extended well beyond their role in the workplace. Self confidence has been given an enormous boost in a number of cases, for many the Wordpower/Numberpower and NVQ Level 2 in Caring certificates were the first certificates they had ever been awarded. The individuals have found many uses for their new or enhanced skills outside work.

Company J

Employer Context

Company J is a manufacturer of waterworks valves and fittings, employing just over 420 employees. Approximately 320 of the employees are shop floor workers and about 100 people work in supervisory and administrative occupations, including a significant number from the Yemeni community.

How need came to be identified

Although the management had not undertaken any formal assessment of the perceived literacy problems, it was felt that generally the ability of the Yemeni workers with English, particularly written skills, was quite poor. Because most of the workers are long serving (15 -20 years of service) this is an impression built up over time.

The Works Manager recognised that the company and individuals would benefit from some training on basic language skills. However, this was not a priority and it was only the approach from the TEC which spurred the training. The Company heard about the project through its link with the local TEC. Company management thought it would be particularly of use to Yemeni and Asian workers within the factory whose English is "not very good".

The employees involves

Around 35-40 of the workforce are from linguistic minority backgrounds. There is a sizeable group of about 30 Yemeni workers and another small group who are of Asian origin. They all work in semi-skilled manual jobs.

Difficulties experienced by the company and individuals before the training took place

There were no particular difficulties experienced by the company which affected production. Managers at the company felt that literacy training would improve the ability of Yemeni and Asian workers to read and understand company notices and memos, although this had not been identified as a major problem.

The workers of Yemeni background are a close-knit community who live together and return to the Yemen only every two or three years to visit their wives and families. They got on well with the rest of the workforce although they had a tendency to revert to their mother tongue amongst themselves. Since the basic skills course started they talk more in English within their group.

The Design of the Training

After Company J decided to participate in the scheme, a local provider was chosen because there was an historic link from previous training. Notices were placed around the factory inviting participants. Encouragement to put themselves forward was given to those from linguistic minorities by managers.

A list of names was given to the provider and a room for tuition made available. The tutor undertook informal individual assessments before the start of the training. The company requested an emphasis on reading.

The tuition was done in company time and workers were paid overtime if necessary. Tuition was in small groups of about 5. Most of the participants were native Yemenis; a couple originally came from Pakistan and one was a white Englishman. It is possible that existing links with the local colleges may have led the company to act if they had offered a similar course. The company was not sure of what type of courses were on offer.

The impact which the training had on individuals' performance at work and the aggregate impact on company performance

The participants reportedly were very enthusiastic and all but one of those who started completed the programme. This surprised the Works Manager who expected a high drop-out rate.

The personal benefits to the individuals involved probably exceed the direct benefits to the company. Greater competence with the English language has led to greater ability to deal with domestic paperwork such as bills and forms. Self-confidence has also grown. The Works Manager reported that there appears to be progress in terms of the interpretation of written instructions, although he was not able to offer any hard evidence or examples.

Overall it is very difficult to assess the contribution to the firm's performance. It is impossible to estimate in cash terms the benefits of the scheme. Subtle longer-term improvements might help production. Health and safety awareness may improve.

It is likely that there are a number of workers of English origin who would benefit from basic skills training. The Works Manager felt that they are perhaps too embarrassed to volunteer. However, it is unlikely that the issue will be addressed – "they cannot be made to participate".

The externally funded course finished in July 1994, but the company had negotiated with the TEC who funded a subsequent extension. The company may fund further extensions to the training if it is reviewed as being successful.

Unforseen benefits/ disbenefits of the training

The company already had good contacts with local training providers and with the TEC. These contacts were exploited for the benefit of the BSAW programme. The BSAW project has consolidated these links.

Practical issues of delivery

Although training was undertaken during works time, 1 hour per week for each worker was easy to accommodate without significant loss of production since those attending the training tended to be from different departments/sections.

Costs

The costs to the firm were said to be too minimal to be of any concern.

Overall comments on usefulness and effectiveness

The programme at Company J appeared to be based on what might be termed a paternalistic approach from management: it was not driven by a calculation of the tangible benefits to the company that may be derived from the training. In a large company such as this, it is not too difficult to release staff from production to undertake training so the costs to the firm are considered to be minimal. It is assumed therefore that the training must be of some good and because the costs are negligible then it is a worthwhile venture.

These assumptions on the part of the management may be accurate. It is certainly difficult to calculate the effect on "the bottom line" of such training although improving communication within an organisation usually produces benefits, many of which are difficult to foresee.

Company Q

Company Q is a manufacturer of specialist cardboard packaging and cartons. There are two plants on one site employing, in total, just over 260 employees. Out of the total workforce of 260, 180 are shop floor production workers. There was a recent history of change within the company involving restructuring, redundancies and redeployment of staff.

How need came to be identified

General improvements to the business over the previous two to three years, such as the introduction of cell working and efforts to promote a cultural change leading to "empowerment" of the workforce, had highlighted some individual basic skills weaknesses. A very poorly written accident report had drawn the attention of senior managers to an individual problem. However, prior to their involvement with a local college initiative designed to help them assess their training needs the company was unaware of any widespread basic skills needs amongst the workforce. Without this initial approach from the college it is unlikely that such a broadly based approach to addressing basic skill needs would have been developed.

The employees involved

The training involved 17 production operatives.

Difficulties experienced by the company and individuals before the training took place

The company had not experienced any specific problems before the start of the training except for the incident involving the badly written accident report (as above). However, there was a general feeling amongst senior management that communication needed to improve in order to facilitate the new culture of "empowerment" of the workforce.

The design of training

The design of the training was largely left to the external tutors, although the company's training co-ordinator asked for an emphasis on communication skills. The company provided a training room and agreed for the training to take place in work time.

The impact which the training had on individuals' performance at work and the aggregate impact on company performance

The feedback from the participants was very enthusiastic, all 17 had completed the programme but qualifications had not been awarded at the time of the research. (A National Record of Achievement will be awarded).

A machine operator reported that the training had "got my brain working again". The personal benefits to the individuals involved probably exceed the direct benefits to the company. One participant has now got a taste for self-improvement and has joined a night class in hair and beauty as a result of the programme. The only direct benefit of the training to the company that the shop-floor staff could identify was an improved ability to deal with paperwork.

The Production Director believes that the contribution to the performance of the company is very difficult to quantify but will be one of several factors helping to improve the culture of "empowerment". The company saw empowerment as giving production operatives greater responsibility for quality and production outputs. It is expected that the basic skills training will contribute to improvements in work performance either directly (better numeracy or literacy skills) or indirectly through greater motivation and commitment.

Unforeseen benefits/ drawbacks of the training

There were no unforeseen benefits or drawbacks identified.

Practical issues of delivery

The training took place in 3 hour blocks, once a week over three or four months. Length varied according to individual need. Delivery took place on site during works time. Compared to the size of the workforce take-up was relatively small and spread across the factory. Therefore there were minimal problems for covering the work of staff absent because of the training.

At the start of the project the management took the decision to ask the shop floor trade union representatives to organise the programme. In the context of recent changes, the management felt that it would be difficult for staff to admit to problems with basic skills without worrying that this admission might single them out for the next phase of redundancies. This was certainly not the motive and indeed the company is at present in the process of expansion and recruiting more staff. However, to allay any suspicions the trade union representatives were given the job of organising the programme "in confidence".

Costs

No costs to the firm had been identified.

Overall comments on usefulness and effectiveness

Despite the commitment to a new management style and a culture of "empowerment" the company still appears to have retained some characteristics of the traditional "us and them" model of employee relations. The staff who participated in the project were pleased with the personal benefits from the training but wanted to know, "what's the company getting out of it?"

The participation rate, considering the ease of availability of the training, was low (less than 10% of the workforce), perhaps showing that there is some way to go before the desired culture is achieved. In order for the company to see real benefits through improvements in communication it would probably require a much higher take-up of the training offered.

Company M

Employer Context

Company M is a small family-run business manufacturing diving equipment and wet suits. In total there are 22 employees and the type of occupations range from designers, administrators and managers through to production workers such as sewing machinists and pattern cutters. Because of the potential dangers involved in diving, the company has to produce a highly reliable product. Quality is therefore a primary issue and to go some way to addressing this, the company is registered for BS 5750.

How need came to be identified

The achievement of BS 5750 was important to the company to help enhance the quality of its product. However, the systems introduced to meet the British Standard generated a lot of written procedures and instructions. It became apparent to managers that two employees in particular, although very competent at their respective jobs, struggled with the paperwork necessary for compliance with BS 5750.

Looking for external help, the Managing Director of Company M contacted a local Community Centre which, amongst other activities provides careers guidance and counselling and training. It is very well known in the local area. Staff at the Centre carried out a skills audit of the whole company to identify training needs in general and also to assess the need for basic skills training.

The employees involves

The skills audit identified two employees who it was thought would benefit from participating in basic skills training. One was a fabric cutter and the other was a production supervisor. Both had problems with basic literacy.

Difficulties experienced by the company and individuals before the training took place

As observed above the key problem for the company was ensuring that all employees complied with the BS 5750 quality systems. In order to be able to complete the necessary paperwork the two employees would have to rely on colleagues to help them. This was clearly an ineffective use of time for the company and "a little embarrassing" for the two people involved.

The cutter, in particular found it difficult to follow any written instructions which would quite often accompany his work. He would rely on colleagues to explain the requirements.

The Design of the Training

Staff from the Community Centre took overall responsibility for the design of the training programme. Wordpower, the City & Guilds qualification in Communication Skills, provided the core of the training for both of the participants, in addition to which the supervisor completed two units of an NVQ level 3 in Supervisory Management. The mode of delivery was for a tutor from the Centre to visit the company on Friday afternoons for a one and a half hour tuition session.

The impact which the training had on individuals' performance at work and the aggregate impact on company performance

The Managing Director reported that the benefits of the basic skills training had been very noticeable. The two people involved were now capable of handling the necessary paperwork for the BS 5750 quality system. They were less reliant on their colleagues for help and thus saved the company time.

The self-confidence of both of the employees had grown. They were both communicating better with their colleagues. The cutter was now more involved with other staff and had picked up more skills. He was thus a more flexible worker.

The supervisor was also better at communicating with other staff. This had improved her ability to supervise effectively. She had also developed a better understanding of the operation of the BS 5750 quality system and its purpose. This meant that she was more able and better motivated to ensure that the system was complied with.

Unforseen benefits/ disbenefits of the training

The context for the training has been strongly work-based. An unanticipated benefit has been derived from the fact that while undertaking coursework based on the organisation the employees have developed a broader understanding of how the company operates. Through contact with the Centre the company has been introduced to Investors in People and is considering working towards the standard.

Practical issues of delivery

The training was delivered out of work time on Friday afternoon after production had finished at lunchtime. The tutor visited the company for the convenience of the employees. The rest-room provided an adequate base for the tuition.

Costs

The employees were paid one and a half hours overtime for attending the tuition. The company viewed this as a worthwhile investment rather than a cost.

Overall comments on usefulness and effectiveness

It is clear that the company is receiving some direct benefits from the training. Time is being saved because the employees involved in the training are now more self-reliant. They are both more competent at their work. The cutter is more flexible and able to deal with a greater variety of work. The supervisor is a more effective communicator and also has a clearer understanding of the BS 5750 quality system. Measuring these benefits in monetary terms is, however, problematic although it may be assumed that the benefits do translate into lower production costs and improved quality. On-site provision of tuition to only two employees for one and a half hours per week is a costly exercise compared with sending them to the local adult education centre. This consideration is probably off-set by the very clear benefits to the company and the individuals involved in this case.

Company P

Company P is a manufacturer of sugar confectionary employing about 500 employees. A further 180 people are employed at their distribution plant nearby.

How need came to be identified

A partnership involving the local TEC, the Local Education Authority and local College was established to promote the BSAW Pilot programme. The major employers in the area were targeted as possible participants in the programme.

Although the management at Company P had not undertaken any formal assessment of basic skills problems, when the company was approached through the local partnership it was felt that employees and the company would benefit from taking part. Generally the progressive introduction of new technology and new working methods has required higher levels of numeracy and communication skills.

The employees involved

In total, 70 staff were involved in the programme which began in September 1993. The shop-floor supervisors (16 "Group Leaders") were the first group of employees to undertake training. They volunteered for help because of increased paperwork associated with their work and also they felt they needed literacy support to assist with study for the Food Hygiene Certificate. The majority of the other staff involved in the programme were shop floor production line operatives plus 3 laboratory workers.

Difficulties experienced by the company and individuals before the training took place

There were no specific difficulties experienced by the company which affected production before the training programme. However, managers at the company felt that general communication could be improved by sessions on writing reports, conduct at meetings, taking minutes and writing memos. The Personnel Manager took the view that the main problem was a lack of confidence rather than skills.

The design of training

Following the agreement of the company management to participate in the programme a training needs assessment was undertaken for the shopfloor staff. Initially 70 staff volunteered to take part. The company provided a room for the training and agreed that the sessions should take place during works time.

A flexible programme of delivery was agreed with the tutors in order to accommodate the company shift patterns. Training was delivered in small groups of 7/8 for 2 hours per week. The only specific requirement from the company was that support should help the supervisors to qualify for the intermediate Food Hygiene certificate.

The impact which the training had on individuals' performance at work and the aggregate impact on company performance

At the time of our visit the company was in the process of undertaking its own evaluation of the programme. Initial feedback from the participants in the programme has been very positive. The supervisors have reported that the operatives appear to have a greater understanding of the production process which helps them in their work. There has been an increase in the number of suggestions for improvements channelled through he company's suggestions scheme. The Personnel Manager reports that, in general, the self-confidence of the production staff and the supervisors involved has increased.

Overall it is difficult to assess the contribution to the firm's performance. Following the completion of the evaluation process it will probably be possible to identify tangible benefits although to estimate benefits in cash terms may be difficult. The scheme will not increase the Company's commitment to training more generally although it has raised awareness of the need for training in basic skills. A further 30 staff are due to join the programme.

Unforeseen benefits/ drawbacks of the training

An unforeseen benefit has been for individuals in their home life. Anecdotal reports to the personnel manager are that staff are more able to help children with their homework and one participant in the training wrote a highly effective letter of complaint.

Practical issues of delivery

The training has been during work time, 2 hours per week for up to 60 workers in one week. Employees work shifts and thus the delivery of the training has been arranged to suit the times of the shifts and people swapping shifts.

Cover has been arranged for staff undertaking training and overtime working has been necessary in some cases.

Costs

The costs to the firm were estimated to be between £2,500 to £3,000 per month – mainly the costs of overtime.

Overall comments on usefulness and effectiveness

Overall, the initial feedback from both the company management and the staff participating in the programme has been positive. At the time of the survey it was reported that a full internal evaluation of the costs and benefits of the programme would be completed by the end of October 1994. However, on the basis of initial findings, the company was planning to continue the basic skills training with a further 30 staff joining the programme in October 1994.

By running the programme during work time the company have committed large amount of resources to the programme, probably around £25,000 in overtime payments alone. This is a large expense and explains the need to formally evaluate the benefits of the programme in order to assess overall effectiveness.

Company I

Employer context

Company I have 3,200 employees (mostly part time). They provide cleaning services at large sites throughout the Greater London area.

How need came to be identified

Company I had already worked with the local TEC on business planning and IIP. Letter writing for managers emerged as a training need in discussions about the possible benefits of basic skills training.

The employees involves

Forty managers at Company I supervise teams of cleaners at the various sites. A majority are male. They have a lot of practical experience, often having "come up the hard way" but they lacked basic skills having left school at 15. They had viewed the course with some anxiety but were soon won over – the tutor was very highly regarded.

Difficulties experienced by the company and individuals before the training took place

The paperwork tasks they are required to carry out include record-keeping, internal memos to colleagues and letters to customers. While most of their work is carried out on site, the managers share office space at Head Office. They preferred telephone and face-to-face conversation to letters. When letter writing was inevitable they tended to seek the help of the training manager, office staff and even the managing director for proof reading or even re-drafting, a time consuming and ultimately costly process ("I would spend half my time doing their jobs!" as one put it).

The difficulties identified by the management and employees prior to the training included: poor spelling; limited knowledge of grammar and limited vocabulary; uncertainty about formats/style of letters and memos, lack of confidence.

The Design of the Training	Short courses of 15 hours in letter writing were provided to groups of about 6 managers. Out of 29 participants, 27 achieved the writing element in City & Guilds 3793 Communications Skills (Wordpower) Stage 1. The training was provided by the nearby Adult College. The suitability of the managers for the training was assessed by the Training Manager who had personal knowledge of them and wrote a brief report on them to the tutor. The tutor then identified individual needs at the beginning of the course.
	The course content was very much work-related with customised templates designed around a "company style" etc. It was designed to help people produce memos, business letters with underpinning skills in grammar, punctuation and spelling. The duration of the course depended on individual ability but all sessions lasted three hours in company time. They were held in the company's training area.
The impact which the training had on individuals' performance at work and the aggregate impact on company performance	According to management and the employees: greatly improved confidence and ability to communicate, more reporting, less demands on senior management to correct work, widened vocabulary (they happily use a thesaurus, as several pointed out), more willingness to help those in similar difficulties (less embarrassment – happy to ask "what's the word for this?"), closer teamwork, better understanding of what is required.
	The company took pleasure in the enthusiasm of the employees and the acceptance of this form of training through word of mouth recommendation
Unforseen benefits/ disbenefits of the training	Contributed to the achievement of BS5750 because managers were more prepared/able to assimilate the procedures.
Practical issues of delivery	There were no significant problems from senior management point of view, but it was a little difficult for employees because it displaced work into the remaining time: "More hours would have caused a problem" and, "I got behind a few times" but generally they organised around it.
Costs	The total cost to the company was identified under the following headings: planning, identification of learners, marketing to learners, organisation, progress meetings, cost of releasing staff (lost productivity, replacement staff, overtime) and amounted to £6.4K.

Longer-term impact

It's helped attitudes in the company (the secretaries now want similar training), but they had a high commitment to training anyway. They are seeking IIP and want to introduce NVQs for their cleaners. They have "training needs coming out of our ears!"

Perceptions of the programme

Management, employees, the training provider and the TEC are uniformly positive about the scheme and its impact. The flexibility and thoroughness of the training provider was particularly highly rated. The college identified 4 reasons for its success: (i) it was adapted to the company's needs; (ii) tutors had experience of working in industry; (iii) it was monitored properly, they kept in touch and reviewed progress; and (iv) they were able to be highly flexible, eg swapping times to meet company needs. Employees were enthusiastic: "Not every course would (help me in future) but this one did; the course was brilliant, I really enjoyed it".

Overall comments on usefulness and effectiveness

The availability of external finance coupled with advice and help from the TEC was critical. Company I was responsive to the suggestion of basic skills in the workplace and gave the project its full support which, together with the quality and commitment of the College, is the reason for the scheme's unqualified success. A relatively simple scheme, but its success has given a further impetus to training at Company I and strengthened the links between the company, the college and the TEC. In terms of the typology, this fits within the **problem-centred** model, although with shades of the company strategy model. A problem was identified although it would probably not been tackled without the on-going dialogue between Company I and the TEC (who essentially sold them BSAW). The training commitment at Company I may evolve into the company strategy model as IIP is secured. Although it was designed to help individuals perform tasks it was less mechanistic than this possibly implies. It was voluntary although employees were encouraged to attend. It was company centred but benefited the individuals. The impact on company performance is difficult to quantify, but is regarded as beneficial eg. improved teamworking.

Company B

Company B is a bread business with 2,000 employees on 13 sites around the UK. It operates through 4 companies and one of them was visited for this study. It has 1,050 employees. It was acquired in 1991 by a major national food producer and since then the new management have sought to reduce duplication and overlap within the company and introduce the parent company's systems and procedures. They refer to a huge list of problems to be addressed. They got the structure sorted out, but, "It was glaringly obvious that the workforce was a separate entity" – citing the authoritarian approach of the old structure/style and a "blame culture" inherited from the previous owner.

How need came to be identified

It was necessary to introduce a 'Basic Food Safety' standard but management realised in early 1993 that this was impossible – Company B is based in a multi-cultural area and there are around 16 different mother tongues spoken among the workforce. Of the 1000 employees, 200 do not even have a basic level of English, and 200-300 can cope but have fundamental problems holding them back.

The company realised that the workforce's English would have to be improved: "Communications was an impediment to the business progressing". They saw it as the starting point of a communications strategy with the workforce: bottom-up as well as top-down. There was also a "mild paternalistic spin-off to help them cope".

The Basic Food Safety standard "Put on the table the scale of the problem we faced". Employees could not read a PC monitor or calculate a percentage. Line leaders could not do an end of shift report.

Difficulties experienced by the company and individuals before the training took place

Management did not quantify the problem; it was very difficult to do so. They were reliant on line leaders who could communicate with managers and their teams rather than being able to select the most capable and motivated as line leaders. They wanted to be able to drive home day-to-day issues through briefing sessions rather than through memos (which were ineffective) but even this was difficult: "We couldn't get the message across". They wanted to foster some individual responsibility for understanding the requirements of key customers such as M&S – and acting upon them.

Reading and writing were cited as the main problems by the employees interviewed who were mostly line managers.

The design of training

The company sought assistance from the local TEC and from ALBSU through the BSAW Pilot and set up an on-site training facility – the Learning for Life Centre. This is a well-equipped set of mobile huts outside of the main factory building. It is delivered through a partnership with a specialist training company rather than a local college because the latter could not provide the flexibility required eg to cover the night shift. It is a City & Guilds accredited centre.

There are a total of 9 classes which reflect ability levels and shift patterns. No class is larger than 10. Through a contract between line manager, tutor and trainee, the employees are released for 2 hours and are expected to attend for a further 2 hours in their own time. Individuals are interviewed by the personnel manager and the tutor where a written assessment is made (based on ALBSU standards). Line leaders are in the vanguard of the training, probably because this will yield an immediate benefit and secure the subsequent promotion of the training to operatives. Participation is voluntary. Only three had refused to participate out of 90.

Course work is work-based, linked to ALBSU standards and to City & Guilds Communication Skills and numeracy awards. They call it Targeted Training (TT). Individuals do 1-2 units depending on what's needed in their jobs rather than working for the whole award. It is planned to deliver units to 300 people in a 12 month period. It is a roll-on roll off programme.

The impact which the training had on individuals' performance at work and the aggregate impact on company performance	The employees felt the benefits were clear-cut. They all said it helped them with their writing, getting information, with their self confidence and in their lives outside work. Most identified improvements in reading, giving information and communicating instructions. A plant manager said his gross margin was up 10% and there had been a huge reduction in waste with the training being the most identifiable factor. Improvements in confidence, attitudes, co-operation were cited. Another manager mentioned greater conformity to systems, higher quality and greater productivity through better team working and line leaders doing their job properly. If the improvement in quality can be sustained it will have a big impact on company performance.
Unforeseen benefits/ drawbacks of the training	The course has clearly helped to address the blame mentality associated with the previous ownership. Also it has developed staff awareness in the company and got across very subtle messages about commitment and trust.
Practical issues of delivery	Management accept that the business is driven by short-termism: anything that takes people off the production line is generally seen by managers and supervisors to be a problem and there was some negative feeling about this. Management felt that supervisors should have better planning and control systems eg. for absenteeism. It was necessary to "take the short-term pain for the long-term gain". With hindsight they would have probably discussed the purpose of the training more with supervisors. Securing the release of employees has been a problem and small groups are less cost effective as the tutor costs remain the same. This now seems to be improving with the efforts now being made to get the message across to supervisors by the production managers.
Costs	The cost to Company B was calculated at an £82K contribution to staff release (hourly rate x 2 hours per week x 52 weeks x 300 employees). They have not estimated the benefits in cash terms.
Longer-term impact	Basic skills levels have been raised. The programme has encouraged a wider and fuller debate and awareness of training and development and strengthened the company's commitment to it. As one manager put it, "The Learning for Life Centre is part of a wider process and initiative". Sister companies within the company are interested in tapping in to the project and Company B is seeking funds to broaden the scope to include supervisory training.

Perceptions of the programme

Management is very positive about the training. The training co-ordinator felt there was initially scepticism among the workforce, but now people are very keen and eager and there is a better attitude to the company, which is echoed by management. When asked whether the training was worthwhile he said, "Definitely yes! It's made my job easier!".

The employees also praised the training in terms of personal benefit, and also the company in areas such as improved productivity, quality and knowledge of food safety. They had no criticism of the pace or content of the course. The only difficulty seemed to be getting released to attend.

Overall comments on usefulness/ effectiveness

The training at Company B probably falls within the problem-centred model because it developed in response to the take-over of the company by a larger group and its need to improve quality and food safety. It encountered problems in doing this with a multi-ethnic workforce lacking basic skills. The company approached the TEC and ALBSU about its problems and established a facility to deal with them. Although they were concerned to get people to perform tasks more efficiently, there was a paternalistic element, since the company wanted to offer employees training that would be of a wider benefit to them. It was, therefore, company and individual centred. The impact on the company was felt to be significant although this had not been formally quantified at the time of the visit. The project had taken longer than expected to get off the ground and it was therefore too early to evaluate in any depth. The training was obviously helping the individuals, but this was often from a very low base and it was clear that they had a long way to go. Perceptions were uniformly positive. The basic skills training was contributing to a wider commitment to training and development and improved management-staff relations.

Company A

Employer context

Company A operates a pool of 12 million pallets which are hired out through its depots to retailers etc. It has 1100 employees of which 600 repair and maintain pallets. It was seeking Investors in People and ISO 9002 and is concerned to meet increasing quality requirements and to contain costs.

How need came to be identified

There was a need to improve the quality of pallets as customer expectations/requirements rise/change. The Company also wanted to introduce specialised equipment and Statistical Process Control. If a fork lift truck driver is to transmit data through terminals they had to be able to read the paperwork. They were pro-active in realising that they needed to upgrade basic skills and sought out ALBSU and were fortunate with their partners the local provider, Avon Community Education, Alpha Training and ALBSU – they did not involve the local TEC.

An associated issue was the very high levels of employee turnover.

How need came to be identified

At the depot where the BSAW trial took place there were 11 employees of which 2 were team leaders, 3 cell leaders, 2 fork lift truck drivers and 3 operatives. All were white men. The training took place between October 1993 – March 1994.

Difficulties experienced by the company and individuals before the training took place

Management felt that the lack of basic skills resulted in very poor communications among the workforce, citing an inability to comprehend requirements or complete standard forms. Turnover was very high (with the total cost associated with each departure/subsequent recruitment at £4-6k).

The design of training

Two programmes were delivered by a local provider. It built on work undertaken by an ALBSU-funded external consultant (including a skills audit) and trialed a customised (to Company A) Wordpower Assessment Pack for Repair and Maintenance Operative Training.

Communications Skills training was delivered to eight employees (20 weeks duration x two hours per week). It covered written skills, including spelling, punctuation and writing for work including letter writing, form filling, memos and report writing. It also covered oral skills required for using the telephone, and talking one-to-one and to small groups. It was closely related to Company A's requirements. It is recognised that a lot was attempted in 20 weeks. Six out of eight received City & Guilds Communication Skills certificates (one at foundation level and five at level one). Two received Records of Achievement for gaining part of the City & Guilds award.

Basic numeracy training (termed "Figure It Out") was also delivered to eight employees (six weeks duration – later extended by three sessions to cover charts and graphs at the request of the employees – x two hours per week). A City & Guilds numeracy qualification was not felt to be appropriate as the competencies concentrated too munch on money and not enough on weights, measures, percentages, ratios etc. Figure It Out was therefore shorter than Communications Skills and covered some relevant competencies rather than using a formal assessment framework. Where possible, Company A documentation was used as course material.

The training was held twice weekly at around shift change-over time and the employees had the option of attending an extra two hours in their own time although few did so, attributing this to the demands of a very physically demanding job.

Candidates were selected for each subject area by the Employee Development Manager/Production Manager/external consultant. The company took account of "not only the need but motivation". The initial assessment was undertaken by the provider's project co-ordinator through personal interviews and in more depth by the trainers at the start of their programmes. The training was compared to an "MOT" which would help employees to be "smarter" by helping them to listen/speak to others, write things down, understand notices, understand and use numbers. The MOT was felt to be a useful analogy since it emphasised that the employees would not necessarily be deficient in all areas.

Candidates completed work-based projects as part of the accreditation process on subjects such as nail waste, stringer stripper machine (presumably this has a bearing on the savings identified below). The production manager was extremely enthusiastic about the quality of the projects and the impact on the motivation and confidence of the individuals producing them – "it's there where we've had the greatest success".

The impact which the training had on individuals' performance at work and the aggregate impact on company performance

All those involved completed the programme and, according to management, a noticeable increase in personal confidence and self-esteem was achieved. Work traditionally done by management can now be delegated to lower-level supervision.

There was a wide consensus among the employees about the benefits of the training. Greater self-confidence and ability to communicate were the most important benefits, but they also reported: tangible gains in literacy/numeracy; understanding what they were supposed to do/coping with new systems; (for supervisors) communicating instructions; teamworking; coming up with ideas and suggestions; and life skills.

Specific savings/impacts were identified by Company A resulting from the BSAW project the depot including:

- **Nail stock control saved £1k in five weeks. Annualised this is equivalent to £10k and if repeated nationally would result in savings of £100k.**

- **The commissioning of a stringer stripping machine six weeks ahead of schedule saved £4k.**

- **Reduction in employee turnover at the depot from 24 in 1993 to just three in the first quarter of 1994 (this saves £4-6k per person).**

This decrease in employee turnover is attributed to increased motivation and greater (possibly temporary) belief/commitment to the company in return for the tangible provision of training by management ("it gave the impression that we cared"). It is recognised that the training effort needs to be sustained. The skills audit commissioned by the company did research attitudes among the workforce and management will be keen to see whether they are able to retain more new employees. It has raised expectations of further training among the workforce which may, however, be difficult to satisfy.

Practical issues of delivery

There was disruption as a result of the training ("Yes and the accountants go berserk!" – see allowance below). Those on the morning shift complained that they were very tired when they went onto the course ("It was difficult to switch off") and felt it should have been at the start of the shift.

Costs

Costs recognised in Company A head office show an allowance/subsidy of £3.5k per trainee. Management believe this was recovered through increased motivation alone. In their successful National Training Award application, the Company have costed the call on their resources as £200k compared with a ALBSU contribution of £53k but it is believed that this refers to the programme in its widest sense including the use of an external consultant and the production of the training manuals.

Longer-term impact

Company A have already come a long way. Two years ago none of the 600 pallet operatives received induction training. Now the company has joined its industry lead body M&ETA. An extension of the Basic Skills trial to other depots was under consideration by company directors at the time of the visit. Certainly, the trial has strengthened the company's commitment to training, which was already broadly-based. Cost considerations are, however, a major factor for the company ("It's a penny business"). The BSAW project and its wider efforts have resulted in the company receiving a National Training Award, as mentioned above.

Perceptions of the programme

The Production Manager said "We have had our money back three times over. It's more than worthwhile. I would have to find it from the depot's budget". He went on, "It is not just individuals who have changed. There is an overall impact". They were grateful that ALBSU gave them a degree of freedom – "they left it to us, let us innovate, but I'm detail conscious and I keep to plan". Another management comment was about the absence of any stigma and none was detected in the interviews with the employees.

The employees were uniformly positive about the training. Comments included: "They get better, more consistent work from me"; "It gave management credibility with the workforce...not just a number"; "It put morale back into the workforce"; "Good for the individual and the company"; "Not a classroom format"; "Management now know what we're capable of".

The provider identified the following key issues:

- **Good, open relationship with the employer;**

- **Full backing and support from the Company;**

- **Mix of employees – team/cell leaders as well as operatives helped raise the profile;**

- **Careful, tight management with evaluation built in.**

Overall comments on usefulness/ effectiveness

This was a well planned, well organised and highly effective scheme. The input from the provider was particularly important to its success. BSAW at Company A fits most closely into the **Company Strategy model**. Although the reason for involvement in BSAW was in response to particular problems, it is also part of a wider (and emerging) training commitment. Although the focus of the training was heavily company centred there was a fairly enlightened attitude about the benefits of training generally to the motivation/retention of the workforce and the success of the business. The impact on company performance was felt to be very significant (even bottom line benefits) as well as in terms of teamworking, motivation etc. The individuals involved clearly benefited from the training, both personally and in terms of work performance.

Appendix 1

References and Areas for Further Research

References

ALBSU. 1993a: *Making it Happen: Improving the Basic Skills of the Workforce*, ALBSU

ALBSU. 1993b: *The Cost to Industry: Basic skills and the UK Workforce*, ALBSU

Atkinson, J & Spilsbury, M. 1993: *Basic Skills and Jobs: A report on the basic skills needed at work*. Prepared by the Institute of Manpower Studies on behalf of the Adult Literacy and Basic Skills Unit, ALBSU/IMS

Berry, T H, (1991), *Managing the Total Quality Transformation*, McGraw Hill.

Business Council for Effective Literacy. 1993: *The connection between employee basic skills and productivity*. Workforce and Workplace Literacy Series, BCEL

Carnevale, A P; Gainer, L J; and Meltzer, A S. 1989. *Workplace Basics: The Skills Employers Want*. American Society for Training and Development

Chisman, F P, 1992. *The Missing Link: Workplace Education in Small Business*. Southport Institute for Policy Analysis (US).

Constable, J & McCormick, R. 1987: *The Making of British Managers*, BIM/CBI

Coopers & Lybrand Associates. 1985: *A Challenge to Complacency: Changing Attitudes to Training*, Report to MSC/NEDO

DTI 1994: *Competitiveness – Helping Business to Win*

DTI 1994: *Managing in the '90s series of guidance notes*

Handy, C. 1987: *The Making of Managers*. MSC/NEO/BIM

Hemphill, D F. 1992: *Workplace ESL Literacy in Diverse Small Business Contexts: Final Evaluation Report on Project EXCEL*. Office of Vocational and Adult Education, Washington, DC

Mikulecky, L. 1989: *Second-Chance Basic Skills, In Investing in People*. Department of Labor (US)

National Literacy Secretariat. 1992: *Basic Skills Basic Business*, NLL

Ross, K. 1992. *Training and Evaluation in the Real World of Work*. Research Paper no. 3, School of Continuing Studies, University of Birmingham

Sticht, T G. 1989: *Functional Context Education, In Investing in People*. Department of Labor

Thiel, K K. 1985: *Job-related Basic Skills*. National Institute of Education, Washington, DC

Areas for Further Research

Arising from the conclusions of this report there are a number of critical issues which we suggest merit further research. We have expressed these in the form of a series of questions focused on key areas of basic skills provision in the workplace:

1. We have underlined the significant contribution which large employers can make in providing access to basic skills for large numbers of employees, who would otherwise be deprived of these opportunities. A series of questions arise from this:

    Why do some large employers make this provision and others fail to do so?

    What steps might be taken to encourage more employers to adopt this policy?

    What are the financial costs and benefits of this type of provision? What would be the likely impact of pump priming this sort of provision with public resources, where private employers may be reluctant to fund it on a 100% basis?

2. We have highlighted the relationship between basic skills provision and the successful development and implementation of initiatives such as TQM, IIP and the achievement of "World Class" standards. Arising from this:

    How successful are traditional approaches to training needs analysis in identifying deficiencies in basic skills?

    How can these approaches be refined in order to ensure that the need to provide for basic skills needs is taken fully into account?

    How can the success of the Company Strategy Model be built upon most effectively? Does this mean new and closer relationships between those involved in education, training and management consultancy including the development of quality systems? If so how can this be brought about – for example is there a role for Training and Enterprise Councils and Business Links in this process?

3. How are the above issues being addressed by our leading industrial competitors? Is the low level of awareness of basic skill needs purely a British phenomenon?

4. How should basic skills needs be defined relative to other education/training needs? Is it an absolute or a relative concept? If the latter, then how are requirements likely to change over the next ten to fifteen years?

ALBSU

ALBSU – The Basic Skills Unit, is the national agency for basic skills in England and Wales. ALBSU is a Company Limited by Guarantee and a registered charity.

By basic skills we mean:

the ability to read, write and speak English and use mathematics at a level necessary to function and progress at work and in society in general.

ALBSU's Patron is Her Royal Highness The Princess Royal. Our Chairman is a leading industrialist, Peter Davis.

We are grant aided by the Department for Education (DFE) and the Welsh Office Education Department (WOED) and are charged with:

developing provision designed to improve the standards of proficiency for adults in the areas of literacy and numeracy, and those related basic communication and coping skills without which progress in and towards education, training or employment is impeded.

We:

- *provide consultancy and advice*

- *sponsor development projects*

- *publish teaching material*

- *fund staff training*

- *commission research.*